CHARTBOOK

A Reference Grammar

Betty Schrampfer Azar

PRENTICE HALL REGENTS
Englewood Cliffs, New Jersey 07632

Library of Congress Cataloging-in-Publication Data

Azar, Betty Schrampfer, 1941–
    Chartbook : a reference grammar / Betty Schrampfer Azar.
        p.   cm.
    At head of title: Fundamentals of English grammar: 2nd edition.
    Includes index.
    ISBN 0-13-340704-7
    1. English language--Textbooks for foreign speakers. 2. English
language --Grammar--Problems, exercises, etc.   I. Azar, Betty
Schrampfer, 1941-   Fundamentals of English grammar. II. Title,
PE1128.A965 1995
428.2'4--dc20

Publisher: *Tina B. Carver*
Managing editor, production: *Dominick Mosco*
Editorial/production supervisor: *Janet Johnston*
Editorial assistant: *Shelley Hartle*
Buyer and Scheduler: *Ray Keating*
Cover supervisor: *Merle Krumper*
Cover producer: *Molly Pike Riccardi*
Cover designer: *Joel Mitnick Design*
Interior designer: *Ros Herion Freese*

©1995 by PRENTICE HALL REGENTS
Prentice-Hall, Inc.
A Simon & Schuster Company
Englewood Cliffs, New Jersey 07632

Printed in the United States of America

10 9 8 7 6 5 4 3 2 1

ISBN 0-13-340704-7

Prentice-Hall International (UK) Limited, *London*
Prentice-Hall of Australia Pty. Limited, *Sydney*
Prentice-Hall Canada Inc., *Toronto*
Prentice-Hall Hispanoamericana, S.A., *Mexico*
Prentice-Hall of India Private Limited, *New Delhi*
Prentice-Hall of Japan, Inc., *Tokyo*
Simon & Schuster Asia Pte. Ltd., *Singapore*
Editora Prentice-Hall do Brasil, Ltda., *Rio de Janeiro*

Wild Bill Schrampfer
1903–1994

Contents

Chapter 4   NOUNS AND PRONOUNS

Chapter 5   MODAL AUXILIARIES

Chapter 6 ASKING QUESTIONS

Chapter 7 THE PRESENT PERFECT AND THE PAST PERFECT

Chapter 8 COUNT/NONCOUNT NOUNS AND ARTICLES

Chapter 9 CONNECTING IDEAS

Chapter 10   GERUNDS AND INFINITIVES

Chapter 11   PASSIVE SENTENCES

Chapter 12   ADJECTIVE CLAUSES

Chapter 13 COMPARISONS

Chapter 14 NOUN CLAUSES

Chapter 15 QUOTED SPEECH AND REPORTED SPEECH

Chapter 16 USING *WISH*, USING *IF*

Preface

This *Chartbook* contains examples and explanations of English grammar for intermediate students of English as a second or foreign language. It is intended principally as an accompaniment to the *Workbook* for *Fundamentals of English Grammar*.

The practices in the *Workbook* are cross-referenced to the charts in this book. This handbook-workbook combination is especially suited to teaching situations where the students need to do much practicing and studying on their own outside the classroom. The *Workbook* contains numerous Selfstudy Practices with the answers given. In addition, Guided Study Practices in the *Workbook* provide ample supplementary classroom materials, with the *Chartbook* serving as a reference text.

The *Teacher's Guide* for *Fundamentals of English Grammar* contains additional notes on many grammar points; each chart is discussed and amplified. Transparencies of the charts are also available under separate cover.

Acknowledgments

I must express my great appreciation to Shelley Hartle, my editorial assistant and good friend. A joy to work with, she handles the many detailed, demanding tasks of book production with outstanding competence. She has been responsible for putting this project together and seeing it through. Thank you, Shelley.

I am truly fortunate to be able to do my work amid many friends. My special thanks go to Tina Carver, publisher and editor of long standing, and to Janet Johnston, ever-capable and cheerful production editor, who shares my insistence that "things be right!"

Thanks also go to the two original editors of *Fundamentals:* colleagues Barbara Matthies and Irene Juzkiw. My appreciation too goes to Joy Edwards and R.T. Steltz for all their help. A very special thanks goes to Ken Kortlever for his help and support.

I especially thank my husband, Don, and my daughter, Chelsea. I pay special tribute to my recently deceased father, William, an educator and text author himself, who always supported whatever paths I've chosen on my way through life.

Betty S. Azar
Langley, Washington

CHAPTER **1**

Present Time

1-1 THE SIMPLE PRESENT AND THE PRESENT PROGRESSIVE

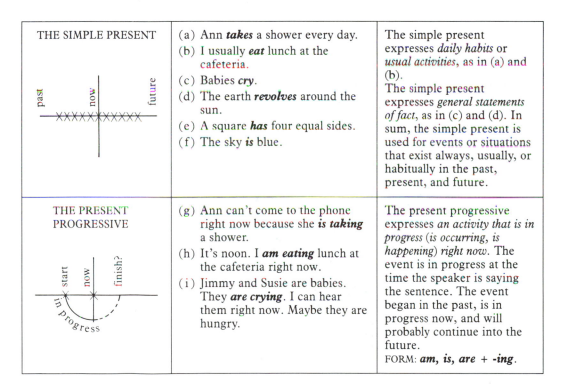

THE SIMPLE PRESENT	(a) Ann **takes** a shower every day.	The simple present expresses *daily habits* or *usual activities*, as in (a) and (b).
	(b) I usually **eat** lunch at the cafeteria.	
	(c) Babies **cry**.	The simple present expresses *general statements of fact*, as in (c) and (d). In sum, the simple present is used for events or situations that exist always, usually, or habitually in the past, present, and future.
	(d) The earth **revolves** around the sun.	
	(e) A square **has** four equal sides.	
	(f) The sky **is** blue.	
THE PRESENT PROGRESSIVE	(g) Ann can't come to the phone right now because she **is taking** a shower.	The present progressive expresses *an activity that is in progress (is occurring, is happening) right now*. The event is in progress at the time the speaker is saying the sentence. The event began in the past, is in progress now, and will probably continue into the future. FORM: **am, is, are + -ing**.
	(h) It's noon. I **am eating** lunch at the cafeteria right now.	
	(i) Jimmy and Susie are babies. They **are crying**. I can hear them right now. Maybe they are hungry.	

1-2 FORMS OF THE SIMPLE PRESENT AND PRESENT PROGRESSIVE

	SIMPLE PRESENT	PRESENT PROGRESSIVE
STATEMENT:	{I-You-We-They} **work.** {He-She-It} **works.**	I **am working.** * {You-We-They} **are working**. {He-She-It} **is working**.
NEGATIVE:	{I-You-We-They} **do not work.** ** {He-She-It} **does not work.**	I **am not working.** {You-We-They} **are not working.** ** {He-She-It} **is not working.**
QUESTION:	**Do** {I-you-we-they} **work?** **Does** {he-she-it} **work?**	**Am** I **working?** **Are** {you-we-they} **working?** **Is** {he-she-it} **working?**

  * Contractions of pronouns with **be**: *I'm, you're, we're, they're, he's, she's, it's.*

 ** Contractions of verbs with **not**: *don't, doesn't, aren't, isn't.* (Note: *am* and *not* are not contracted.)

SIMPLE PRESENT:
Mrs. Wilson **reads** the newspaper *every morning.*
Mr. Wilson usually **pours** his own coffee *in the morning.*
The children **play** with their toys *every day* before
they go to school.

PRESENT PROGRESSIVE:
Right now Mrs. Wilson **is reading** the newspaper.
Mr. Wilson **is pouring** a cup of coffee. The children
are playing with their toys.

1-3 SPELLING: FINAL -S vs. -ES

(a) visit → visit**s** answer → answer**s** speak → speak**s** happen → happen**s**	Final **-s**, not **-es**, is added to most verbs. (INCORRECT: *visites, speakes, answeres, happenes*)
(b) hope → hope**s** write → write**s**	Many verbs end in **-e**. Final **-s** is simply added.

(c) catch → catch**es**   fix → fix**es**
    wash → wash**es**   buzz → buzz**es**
    pass → pass**es**
	Final **-es** is added if the verb ends in **-ch, -sh, -s, -x,** or **-z.**

(d) do → do**es** go → go**es**	Final **-es** is added to **do** and **go**.
(e) study → stud**ies** try → tr**ies**	If a verb ends in a consonant + **-y**, change the **-y** to **-i** and add **-es**. (INCORRECT: *studys*)
(f) pay → pay**s** buy → buy**s**	If a verb ends in a vowel* + **-y**, simply add **-s** (INCORRECT: *paies* or *payes*)

* Vowels = *a, e, i, o, u*. Consonants = all the other letters in the alphabet.

1-4 NONPROGRESSIVE VERBS

(a) I **hear** a bird. It is singing. (b) I'm hungry. I **want** a sandwich. (c) This book **belongs** to Mikhail.	Some verbs are not used in progressive tenses. CORRECT: *I hear a bird (right now).* INCORRECT: *I am hearing a bird (right now).*

NONPROGRESSIVE VERBS

hear	believe	be	own	need	like	forget
see	think*	exist	have*	want	love	remember
	understand		possess	prefer	hate	
	know		belong			

* Sometimes *think* and *have* are used in progressive tenses.
  COMPARE:
  *I **think** that grammar is easy.* → When **think** means **believe**, it is nonprogressive.
  *I **am thinking** about grammar right now.* → When **think** expresses thoughts that are going through a person's mind, it can be progressive.
  *Tom **has** a car.* → When **have** expresses possession, it is not used in the present progressive.
  *I'm **having** a good time.* → In certain idiomatic expressions (e.g., *have a good time*), **have** can be used in the present progressive.

1-5 SIMPLE PRESENT AND PRESENT PROGRESSIVE: SHORT ANSWERS TO QUESTIONS

	QUESTION	SHORT ANSWER	LONG ANSWER
SIMPLE PRESENT	*Does* Bob *like* tea?	Yes, he **does**. No, he **doesn't**.	Yes, he *likes* tea. No, he *doesn't like* tea.
	Do you *like* tea?	Yes, I **do**. No, I **don't**.	Yes, I *like* tea. No, I *don't like* tea.
PRESENT PRO-GRESSIVE	*Are* you *studying*?	Yes, I **am**.★ No, I**'m not**.	Yes, I *am studying*. No, I*'m not studying*.
	Is Yoko *studying*?	Yes, she **is**.★ No, she**'s not**. OR: No, she **isn't**.	Yes, she *is studying*. No, she*'s not studying*. OR: No, she *isn't studying*.
	Are they *studying*?	Yes, they **are**.★ No, they**'re not**. OR: No, they **aren't**.	Yes, they*'re studying*. No, they*'re not* studying. OR: No, they *aren't studying*.

★ *Am, is,* and *are* are not contracted with pronouns in short answers.
INCORRECT SHORT ANSWERS: *Yes, I'm. Yes, she's. Yes, they're.*

Is Jean **studying** at the library this evening?
No, she **isn't**. She *isn't studying* at the library
this evening. She's at the student union.
She's playing pool with her friend.

CHAPTER **2**
Past Time

2-1 EXPRESSING PAST TIME: THE SIMPLE PAST

(a) Mary **walked** downtown yesterday. (b) I **slept** for eight hours last night.	The simple past is used to talk about activities or situations that began and ended in the past (e.g., *yesterday, last night, two days ago, in 1990*).
(c) Bob **stayed** home yesterday morning. (d) Our plane **arrived** on time.	Most simple past verbs are formed by adding **-ed** to a verb, as in (a), (c), and (d).
(e) I **ate** breakfast this morning. (f) Sue **took** a taxi to the airport.	Some verbs have irregular past forms, as in (b), (e), and (f). See Chart 2-4.

2-2 FORMS OF THE SIMPLE PAST

STATEMENT	{ I - You - She - He - It - We - They }	**worked** yesterday. **ate** breakfast.
NEGATIVE*	{ I - You - She - He - It - We - They }	**did not** (**didn't**) **work** yesterday. **did not** (**didn't**) **eat** breakfast.
QUESTION*	**Did** { I - you - she - he - it - we - they }	**work** yesterday? **eat** breakfast?
SHORT ANSWER	Yes, No, { I - you - she - he - it - we - they }	**did**. **didn't**.

* NOTE: *Did* is NOT used with *was* and *were*.

    NEGATIVE: { I - She - He - It } **was not** (**wasn't**) busy.
                    { We - You - They } **were not** (**weren't**) busy.
    QUESTION: **Was** { I - she - he - it } right?
                Were { we - you - they } right?

2-3 THE PRINCIPAL PARTS OF A VERB

	SIMPLE FORM	SIMPLE PAST	PAST PARTICIPLE	PRESENT PARTICIPLE
REGULAR VERBS	finish stop hope wait play try	finished stopped hoped waited played tried	finished stopped hoped waited played tried	finishing stopping hoping waiting playing trying
IRREGULAR VERBS	see make sing eat put go	saw made sang ate put went	seen made sung eaten put gone	seeing making singing eating putting going
PRINCIPAL PARTS OF A VERB: (1) the simple form	English verbs have four principal forms or ''parts.'' **The simple form** is the form that is found in a dictionary. It is the base form with no endings on it (no final *-s*, *-ed*, or *-ing*).			
(2) the simple past	**The simple past** form ends in *-ed* for regular verbs. Most verbs are regular, but many common verbs have irregular past forms. See the reference list of irregular verbs that follows in Chart 2-4.			
(3) the past participle	**The past participle** also ends in *-ed* for regular verbs. Some verbs are irregular. It is used in perfect tenses (Chapter 7) and the passive (Chapter 12).			
(4) the present participle	**The present participle** ends in *-ing* (for both regular and irregular verbs). It is used in progressive tenses (e.g., the present progressive and the past progressive).			

People often *eat* ice cream and cake for dessert.
I *ate* some ice cream yesterday.
I've *eaten* ice cream many times in my lifetime.
The woman in the picture is *eating* ice cream.

SIMPLE FORM	SIMPLE PAST	PAST PARTICIPLE	SIMPLE FORM	SIMPLE PAST	PAST PARTICIPLE
be	was, were	been	lie	lay	lain
become	became	become	light	lit (lighted)	lit (lighted)
begin	began	begun	lose	lost	lost
bend	bent	bent	make	made	made
bite	bit	bitten	mean	meant	meant
blow	blew	blown	meet	met	met
break	broke	broken	pay	paid	paid
bring	brought	brought	put	put	put
broadcast	broadcast	broadcast	quit	quit	quit
build	built	built	read	read	read
buy	bought	bought	ride	rode	ridden
catch	caught	caught	ring	rang	rung
choose	chose	chosen	rise	rose	risen
come	came	come	run	ran	run
cost	cost	cost	say	said	said
cut	cut	cut	see	saw	seen
dig	dug	dug	sell	sold	sold
do	did	done	send	sent	sent
draw	drew	drawn	set	set	set
drink	drank	drunk	shake	shook	shaken
drive	drove	driven	shoot	shot	shot
eat	ate	eaten	shut	shut	shut
fall	fell	fallen	sing	sang	sung
feed	fed	fed	sit	sat	sat
feel	felt	felt	sleep	slept	slept
fight	fought	fought	slide	slid	slid
find	found	found	speak	spoke	spoken
fit	fit	fit	spend	spent	spent
fly	flew	flown	spread	spread	spread
forget	forgot	forgotten	stand	stood	stood
forgive	forgave	forgiven	steal	stole	stolen
freeze	froze	frozen	stick	stuck	stuck
get	got	gotten (got)	strike	struck	struck
give	gave	given	swear	swore	sworn
go	went	gone	sweep	swept	swept
grow	grew	grown	swim	swam	swum
hang	hung	hung	take	took	taken
have	had	had	teach	taught	taught
hear	heard	heard	tear	tore	torn
hide	hid	hidden	tell	told	told
hit	hit	hit	think	thought	thought
hold	held	held	throw	threw	thrown
hurt	hurt	hurt	understand	understood	understood
keep	kept	kept	upset	upset	upset
know	knew	known	wake	woke	waked (woken)
lay	laid	laid	wear	wore	worn
lead	led	led	win	won	won
leave	left	left	withdraw	withdrew	withdrawn
lend	lent	lent	write	wrote	written
let	let	let			

2-5 SPELLING OF -*ING* AND -*ED* FORMS

END OF VERB	DOUBLE THE CONSONANT?	SIMPLE FORM	-*ING*	-*ED*	
-*e*	NO	(a) smile hope	smiling hoping	smiled hoped	-*ing* form: Drop the -*e*, add -*ing*. -*ed* form: Just add -*d*.
Two Consonants	NO	(b) help learn	helping learning	helped learned	If the verb ends in two consonants, just add -*ing* or -*ed*.
Two Vowels + One Consonant	NO	(c) rain heat	raining heating	rained heated	If the verb ends in two vowels + a consonant, just add -*ing* or -*ed*.
One Vowel + One Consonant	YES	ONE-SYLLABLE VERBS (d) stop plan	stopping planning	stopped planned	If the verb has one syllable and ends in one vowel + one consonant, double the consonant to make the –*ing* or –*ed* form.*
	NO	TWO-SYLLABLE VERBS (e) vísit óffer	visiting offering	visited offered	If the first syllable of a two-syllable verb is stressed, do not double the consonant.
	YES	(f) preférr admít	preferring admitting	preferred admitted	If the second syllable of a two-syllable verb is stressed, double the consonant.
-*y*	NO	(g) play enjoy	playing enjoying	played enjoyed	If the verb ends in a vowel + -*y*, keep the -*y*. Do not change it to -*i*.
		(h) worry study	worrying studying	worried studied	If the verb ends in a consonant + -*y*, keep the -*y* for the -*ing* form, but change the -*y* to -*i* to make the -*ed* form.
-*ie*		(i) die tie	dying tying	died tied	-*ing* form: Change -*ie* to -*y* and add -*ing*. -*ed* form: Just add -*d*.

* Exceptions: Do not double *w* or *x*: *snow, snowing, snowed*
fix, fixing, fixed

2-6 THE SIMPLE PAST AND THE PAST PROGRESSIVE

THE SIMPLE PAST	(a) Mary **walked** downtown yesterday. (b) I **slept** for eight hours last night.	The simple past is used to talk about activities or situations that **began and ended** at a particular time in the past (e.g., *yesterday, last night, two days ago, in 1990*), as in (a) and (b).
THE PAST PROGRESSIVE	(c) I sat down at the dinner table at 6:00 P.M. yesterday. Tom came to my house at 6:10 P.M. I **was eating** dinner when Tom came. (d) I went to bed at 10:00. The phone rang at 11:00. I **was sleeping** when the phone rang.	The past progressive expresses an activity that **was in progress** (was occurring, was happening) at a point of time in the past (e.g., *at 6:10*) or at the time of another action (e.g., *when Tom came.*) In (c): Eating was in progress at 6:10; eating was in progress when Tom came. FORM: **was, were + -ing**.
(e) **When** *the phone rang*, I was sleeping. (f) The phone rang **while** *I was sleeping*.		**when** = at that time **while** = during that time (e) and (f) have the same meaning.
(g) *While* I **was doing** my homework, my roommate **was watching** TV.		In (g): When two actions are in progress at the same time, the past progressive can be used in both parts of the sentence.

2-7 FORMS OF THE PAST PROGRESSIVE

STATEMENT	{I-She-He-It} *was working*. {You-We-They} *were working*.
NEGATIVE	{I-She-He-It} *was not (wasn't) working*. {You-We-They} *were not (weren't) working*.
QUESTION	*Was* {I-she-he-it} *working*? *Were* {you-we-they} *working*?
SHORT ANSWER	Yes, {I-she-he-it} *was*. No, {I-she-he-it} *wasn't*. Yes, {you-we-they} *were*. No, {you-we-they} *weren't*.

2-8 EXPRESSING PAST TIME: USING TIME CLAUSES

(a) `time clause` *When I went to Chicago,* `main clause` *I visited my uncle.* (b) `main clause` *I visited my uncle* `time clause` *when I went to Chicago.*	*when I went to Chicago* = a time clause★ *I visited my uncle* = a main clause★ (a) and (b) have the same meaning.
	A time clause can: (1) come in front of a main clause, as in (a); (2) follow a main clause, as in (b).
(c) *After Mary ate dinner*, she went to the library. (d) Mary went to the library *after she ate dinner*. (e) *Before I went to bed*, I finished my homework. (f) I finished my homework *before I went to bed*. (g) *While I was watching TV*, the phone rang. (h) The phone rang *while I was watching TV*. (i) *When the phone rang*, I was watching TV. (j) I was watching TV *when the phone rang*.	**When, after, before,** and **while** introduce time clauses. *when* *after* *before* } + subject and verb = a time clause *while*
	PUNCTUATION: Put a comma at the end of a time clause when the time clause comes first in a sentence (comes in front of the main clause): **time clause + comma + main clause** **main clause + NO comma + time clause**
(k) When the phone *rang*, I *answered* it.	In a sentence with a time clause introduced by **when**, both the time clause verb and the main verb can be simple past. In this case, the action in the "**when** clause" happened first. In (i): *First: the phone rang. Then: I answered it.*

★ A *clause* is a structure that has a subject and a verb.

When we got to the park, Larry and I fed the ducks on the pond. One duck caught the bread in midair **before it hit the water.**

2-9 EXPRESSING PAST HABIT: *USED TO*

(a) I **used to live** with my parents. Now I live in my own apartment. (b) Ann **used to be** afraid of dogs, but now she likes dogs. (c) Don **used to smoke**, but he doesn't anymore.	**Used to** expresses a past situation or habit that no longer exists at present. FORM: **used to** + *the simple form of a verb*
(d) **Did** you **use to live** in Paris?	QUESTION FORM: **did** + *subject* + **use to**
(e) I **didn't use to drink** coffee at breakfast. (f) I **never used to drink** coffee at breakfast, but now I always have coffee in the morning.	NEGATIVE FORM: **didn't use to/never used to**

2-10 PREPOSITIONS OF TIME: *IN, AT,* and *ON*

The prepositions *in, at,* and *on* are used in time expressions as follows:	
(a) Please be on time *in the future.* (b) I usually watch TV *in the evening.*	**in the past, in the present, in the future★** **in the morning, in the afternoon, in the evening**
(c) We sleep *at night.* I was asleep *at midnight.* (d) I fell asleep *at 9:30 (nine-thirty).* (e) He's busy *at present.* Please call again.	**at noon, at night, at midnight** **at** + *"clock time"* **at present, at the moment, at the present time**
(f) I was born *in October.* (g) I was born *in 1975.* (h) I was born *in the twentieth century.* (i) The weather is hot *in (the) summer.★★*	**in** + *a month/a year/a century/a season*
(j) I was born *on October 31, 1975.* (k) I went to a movie *on Thursday.* (l) I have class *on Thursday morning(s).*	**on** + *a date/a weekday* **on** + *weekday morning(s), afternoon(s), evening(s)*

★ Possible in British English: *in future. (Please be on time in future.)*

★★ In expressions with the seasons, *the* is optional: *in (the) spring, in (the) summer, in (the) fall/autumn, in (the) winter.*

CHAPTER 3
Future Time

3-1 EXPRESSING FUTURE TIME: *BE GOING TO* AND *WILL*

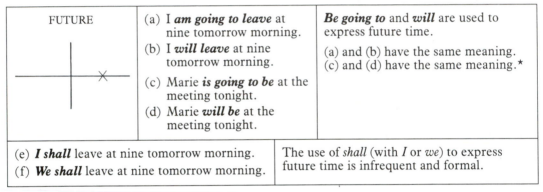

FUTURE	(a) I **am going to leave** at nine tomorrow morning.	**Be going to** and **will** are used to express future time.
	(b) I **will leave** at nine tomorrow morning.	(a) and (b) have the same meaning.
	(c) Marie **is going to be** at the meeting tonight.	(c) and (d) have the same meaning.*
	(d) Marie **will be** at the meeting tonight.	
(e) **I shall** leave at nine tomorrow morning.		The use of *shall* (with *I* or *we*) to express future time is infrequent and formal.
(f) **We shall** leave at nine tomorrow morning.		

* **Will** and **be going to** usually give the same meaning, but sometimes they express different meanings. The differences are discussed in Chart 3-4.

3-2 FORMS WITH *WILL*

STATEMENT	{I-You-She-He-It-We-They} **will come** tomorrow.	
NEGATIVE	{I-You-She-He-It-We-They} **will not** (**won't**) **come** tomorrow.	
QUESTION	**Will** {I-you-she-he-it-we-they} **come** tomorrow?	
SHORT ANSWER	Yes, {I-you-she-he-it-we-they} **will**. No, {I-you-she-he-it-we-they} **won't**.	
CONTRACTIONS	I'll, you'll, she'll, he'll, it'll, we'll, they'll	**Will** is usually contracted with pronouns in both speech and informal writing.
	Bob + will = "Bob'll" the teacher will = "the teacher'll"	**Will** is usually contracted with nouns in speech, but usually not in writing.

3-3 USING *PROBABLY* WITH *WILL*

(a) Ann *will* **probably** *go* to the park tomorrow. (b) Bob **probably** *won't go* to the park tomorrow. (c) FORMAL: Bob *will* **probably** *not go* to the park tomorrow.	People often use **probably** with **will**. **Probably** comes between **will** and the main verb, as in (a). In a negative sentence, **probably** comes in front of **won't**, as in (b), or more formally, between **will** and **not**, as in (c).*

* See Chart 7-8 for more information about placement of midsentence adverbs such as **probably**.

3-4 *BE GOING TO* vs. *WILL*

(a) She *is going to succeed* because she works hard. (b) She *will succeed* because she works hard.	***Be going to*** and ***will*** are the same when they are used to make predictions about the future. (a) and (b) have the same meaning.
(c) I bought some wood because **I am going to build** a bookcase for my apartment.	***Be going to*** (but not ***will***) is used to express a preconceived plan. In (c): The speaker is planning to build a bookcase.
(d) This chair is too heavy for you to carry alone. **I'll help** you.	***Will*** (but not ***be going to***) is used to volunteer or express willingness. In (d): The speaker is happy to help.

Jim is looking at his ice cream cone.
He *is going to eat* it.

3-5 EXPRESSING FUTURE TIME IN TIME CLAUSES AND "IF-CLAUSES"

(a) *Before I **go** to class tomorrow*, I'm going to eat breakfast.	The simple present is used in a future time clause. ***Be going to*** and ***will*** are NOT used in a future time clause.
(b) I'm going to eat dinner at 6:00 tonight. *After I **eat** dinner*, I'm going to study in my room.	*before* *after* *when* } + subject and verb + a time clause★ *as soon as*
(c) I'll give Mary your message *when I **see** her tomorrow*.	In (a): The speaker is talking about two events: going to class and eating breakfast. Both events are in the future. However, the speaker uses the simple present (not ***be going to*** or ***will***) to talk about going to class because the verb occurs in a time clause:
(d) It's raining right now. *As soon as the rain **stops***, I'm going to walk downtown.	*Before I **go** to class tomorrow . . . .*
(e) Maybe it will rain tomorrow. *If it **rains** tomorrow*, I'm going to stay home.	When the meaning is future, the simple present (not ***be going to*** or ***will***) is used in an "if-clause." ***If*** + *subject and verb* = an "if-clause"★

★ See Chapter 16 for other uses of "if-clauses."

Jack is watching a football game on TV right now. *As soon as the game **is** over*, he *will mow* the grass in the back yard.

3-6   PARALLEL VERBS

v *and* **v** (a) Jim **makes** his bed *and* **cleans** up his room every morning.	Often a subject has two verbs that are connected by **and**. We say that the two verbs are parallel: **v** + ***and*** + **v** *makes* *and* *cleans* = parallel verbs
(b) Ann **is cooking** dinner *and* (*is*) **talking** on the phone at the same time. (c) I **will stay** home *and* (*will*) **study** tonight. (d) I **am going to stay** home *and* (*am going to*) **study** tonight.	It is not necessary to repeat a helping verb (an auxiliary verb) when two verbs are connected by **and**.

3-7   USING THE PRESENT PROGRESSIVE TO EXPRESS FUTURE TIME

(a) Don **is going to come** to the party tomorrow night. (b) Don **is coming** to the party tomorrow night. (c) We**'re going to go** to a movie tonight. (d) We**'re going** to a movie tonight. (e) I**'m going to stay** home tonight. (f) I**'m staying** home tonight. (g) Ann **is going to fly** to Chicago next week. (h) Ann **is flying** to Chicago next week. (i) Bob **is going to take** a taxi to the airport tomorrow. (j) Bob **is taking** a taxi to the airport tomorrow.	Sometimes the present progressive is used to express future time. (a) and (b) have the same meaning. The present progressive is used to express future time when the sentence concerns **a definite plan, a definite intention, a definite future activity.** *

(k) A: You shouldn't buy that used car. It's in terrible condition. It costs too much. You don't have enough money. You'll have to get insurance, and you can't afford the insurance. Buying that used car is a crazy idea.
    B: I **am buying** that used car tomorrow morning! My mind is made up. Nobody—not you, not my mother, not my father—can stop me. I**'m buying** that car, and that's it! I don't want to talk about it anymore.
    A: Oh well, it's your money.
	Verbs such as **come**, **go**, **stay**, **arrive**, **leave** are frequently used in the present progressive to express future time. Such verbs express definite plans.
	Verbs expressing planned means of transportation in the future are also frequently used in the present progressive; for example, **fly**, **walk**, **ride**, **drive**, **take** (a bus, a taxi, etc.).
	
	Sometimes a speaker will use the present progressive when he or she wants to make **a very strong statement** about a future activity, as in (k).

* A future meaning for the present progressive is indicated either by future time words in the sentence or by the context.

3-8 USING THE SIMPLE PRESENT TO EXPRESS FUTURE TIME

(a) My plane **arrives** at 7:35 *tomorrow evening*. (b) Tom's new job **starts** *next week*. (c) The semester **ends** *in two more weeks*. (d) There **is** a meeting at ten *tomorrow morning*.	The simple present can express future time when events are on a definite schedule or timetable. Only a few verbs are used in the simple present to express future time. The most common are **arrive**, **leave**, **start**, **begin**, **end**, **finish**, **open**, **close**, **be**.

3-9 PRESENT PLANS FOR FUTURE ACTIVITIES: USING *INTEND*, *PLAN*, *HOPE*

(a) I*'m intending*/I *intend* **to go** to Paris. (b) I*'m planning*/I *plan* **to take** a trip next month. (c) I*'m hoping*/I *hope* **to fly** to Paris next month.	*Intend*, *plan*, and *hope* are used in present tenses to express present ideas about future activities. INCORRECT: *I will intend to go to Paris next month.*
TO + THE SIMPLE FORM OF A VERB (d) I intend **to** + **go** I plan **to** + **take**	*Intend*, *plan*, and *hope* are followed by an infinitive (**to** + the simple form of a verb).*

* See Chapter 10 for more information about infinitives.

3-10 IMMEDIATE FUTURE: USING *BE ABOUT TO*

(a) Ann's bags are packed, and she is wearing her coat. She **is about to leave** for the airport. (b) Shhh. The movie **is about to begin**.	The idiom **be about to do something** expresses an activity that will happen in the **immediate future**, usually within five minutes. In (a): Ann is going to leave sometime in the next few minutes.

Rita is holding a fly swatter and staring at a fly on the kitchen table. She **is about to hit** the fly.

CHAPTER *4*
Nouns and Pronouns

4-1 PLURAL FORMS OF NOUNS

		SINGULAR	PLURAL	
(a)		one bird	two **birds**	To make most nouns plural, add **-s**.
		one street	two **streets**	
		one rose	two **roses**	
(b)		one dish	two **dishes**	Add **-es** to nouns ending in **-sh, -ch, -ss,** and **-x**.
		one match	two **matches**	
		one class	two **classes**	
		one box	two **boxes**	
(c)		one baby	two **babies**	If a noun ends in a consonant + **-y**, change the "**y**" to "**i**" and add **-es**. (NOTE: If **-y** is preceded by a vowel, add only **-s**: *boys, days, keys*.)
		one city	two **cities**	
(d)		one knife	two **knives**	If a noun ends in **-fe** or **-f**, change the ending to **-ves**. (Exceptions: *beliefs, chiefs, roofs, cuffs*.)
		one shelf	two **shelves**	
(e)		one tomato	two **tomatoes**	The plural form of nouns that end in **-o** is sometimes **-oes** and sometimes **-os**.
		one zoo	two **zoos**	**-oes**: *tomatoes, potatoes, heroes, echoes, mosquitoes*
		one zero	two **zeroes** / **zeros**	**-os**: *zoos, radios, studios, pianos, solos, sopranos, photos, autos*
				-oes or -os: *zeroes/zeros, volcanoes/volcanos, tornadoes/tornados*
(f)		one child	two **children**	Some nouns have irregular plural forms. (NOTE: The singular form of *people* can be *person, woman, man, child*. For example, one man and one child = two people.)
		one foot	two **feet**	
		one goose	two **geese**	
		one man	two **men**	
		one mouse	two **mice**	
		one tooth	two **teeth**	
		one woman	two **women**	
		—	two **people**	

(g)	one deer	two **deer**	The plural form of some nouns is the same as the
	one fish	two **fish**	singular form.
	one sheep	two **sheep**	
	one offspring	two **offspring**	
	one species	two **species**	
(h)	one bacterium	two **bacteria**	Some nouns that English has borrowed from other
	one cactus	two **cacti**	languages have foreign plurals.
	one crisis	two **crises**	
	one phenomenon	two **phenomena**	

4-2 SUBJECTS, VERBS, AND OBJECTS

S   V
(a) The **sun shines**.
     (noun) (verb)
 	
S   V
(b) **Plants   grow**.
     (noun)   (verb)
	An English sentence has a SUBJECT (**S**) and a VERB (**V**).
	
	The SUBJECT is a **noun**. In (a): *sun* is a noun; it is the subject of the verb *shines*.

S   V   O
(c) **Plants   need   water**.
     (noun)   (verb) (noun)
 	
S   V   O
(d) **Bob   is reading   a book**.
     (noun)   (verb)   (noun)
	Sometimes a VERB is followed by an OBJECT (**O**).
	
	The OBJECT of a verb is a **noun**. In (c): *water* is the object of the verb *need*.

4-3 OBJECTS OF PREPOSITIONS

S   V   O   PREP   O of PREP
(a) Ann put her books **on**   the **desk**.
                                (noun)
 	
S   V PREP   O of PREP
(b) A leaf fell **to**   the **ground**.
                            (noun)
	Many English sentences have prepositional phrases. In (a): "on the desk" is a prepositional phrase. A prepositional phrase consists of a PREPOSITION (**PREP**) and an OBJECT OF A PREPOSITION (**O of PREP**). The object of a preposition is a *noun*.

REFERENCE LIST OF PREPOSITIONS

about	before	despite	of	to
above	behind	down	off	toward(s)
across	below	during	on	under
after	beneath	for	out	until
against	beside	from	over	up
along	besides	in	since	upon
among	between	into	through	with
around	beyond	like	throughout	within
at	by	near	till	without

4-4   USING ADJECTIVES TO DESCRIBE NOUNS

(a) Bob is reading a **good** *book*. (adjective + noun)	Words that describe nouns are called *adjectives*. In (a): *good* is an adjective; it describes the book.
(b) The **tall** *woman* wore a **new** *dress*. (c) The **short** *woman* wore an **old** *dress*. (d) The **young** *woman* wore a **short** *dress*.	We say that adjectives "modify" nouns. "Modify" means "change a little." An adjective changes the meaning of a noun by giving more information about it.
(e) Roses are **beautiful** *flowers*. INCORRECT: Roses are beautifuls flowers.	Adjectives are neither singular nor plural. They do NOT have a plural form.
(f) He wore a **white** *shirt*. INCORRECT: He wore a shirt white. (g) Roses *are* **beautiful**. (h) His shirt *was* **white**.	Adjectives can come immediately before nouns, as in (f). Adjectives can also follow main verb *be*, as in (g) and (h).

Crocodiles have **big** teeth.

4-5   USING NOUNS AS ADJECTIVES

(a) I have a **flower** *garden*. (b) The **shoe** *store* also sells socks. (c) INCORRECT: a flowers garden INCORRECT: the shoes store	Sometimes words that are usually used as nouns are used as adjectives. For example, *flower* is usually a noun, but in (a) it is used as an adjective to modify *garden*. When a noun is used as an adjective, it is singular in form, NOT plural.

4-6   PERSONAL PRONOUNS: SUBJECTS AND OBJECTS

PERSONAL PRONOUNS					
SUBJECT PRONOUNS:	**I**	**we**	**you**	**she, he, it**	**they**
OBJECT PRONOUNS:	**me**	**us**	**you**	**her, him, it**	**them**

S (a) ***Kate*** is married. ***She*** has two children.	A pronoun refers to a noun. It is used in place of a noun. In (a): "she" is a pronoun. It refers to "Kate." It is used in place of the noun "Kate." In (b): "her" is a pronoun. It refers to "Kate." ***She*** is a subject pronoun; ***her*** is an object pronoun. A pronoun is used in the same ways as a noun: as a subject or as an object of a verb or preposition.
O (b) ***Kate*** is my friend. I know ***her*** well.	
(c) Mike has ***a new blue bicycle***. He bought ***it*** yesterday.	A pronoun can refer to a single noun, as in (a) and (b). A pronoun can also refer to a noun phrase. In (c): "it" refers to the whole noun phrase "a new blue bicycle."
S (d) *[Eric and I]* are good friends. O (e) Ann met *[Eric and me]* at the museum. O of **PREP** (f) Ann walked between *[Eric and me]*.	Sometimes nouns and pronouns are connected by ***and***. The choice of a pronoun after ***and*** can be troublesome.* If the pronoun is used as part of the subject, use a subject pronoun (e.g., *I*), as in (d). If it is part of the object, use an object pronoun, (e.g., *me*) as in (e) and (f).

SINGULAR PRONOUNS:	**I**	**me**	**you**	**she, he, it**	**her, him**
PLURAL PRONOUNS:	**we**	**us**	**you**	**they**	**them**

(g) ***Mike*** is in class. ***He*** is taking a test. (h) The ***students*** are in class. ***They*** are taking a test. (i) ***Kate and Tom*** are married. ***They*** have two children.	*Singular* = one. *Plural* = more than one. Singular pronouns refer to singular nouns, plural pronouns to plural nouns. In (g): "Mike" is singular (one person), so a singular pronoun (*he*) is used. In (h): "students" is plural, so a plural pronoun (*they*) is used.

*Pronoun usage after ***and*** can be troublesome for native speakers, too!

Mr. Edwards is looking at ***his new tie***.
He bought ***it*** yesterday.

4-7 POSSESSIVE NOUNS

SINGULAR: (a) I know the **student's** name. PLURAL: (b) I know the **students'** names. PLURAL: (c) I know the **children's** names.		An apostrophe (') and an **-s** are used with nouns to show possession. Notice the patterns:

SINGULAR	the student ⟶ the **student's** name my baby ⟶ my **baby's** name a man ⟶ a **man's** name	SINGULAR POSSESSIVE NOUN: noun + apostrophe (') + **-s**

PLURAL	the students ⟶ the **students'** names
	my babies ⟶ my **babies'** names
	men ⟶ **men's** names
	the children ⟶ the **children's** names
		PLURAL POSSESSIVE NOUN:
		   noun + **-s** + apostrophe (')
		IRREGULAR PLURAL* POSSESSIVE NOUN:
		   noun + apostrophe (') + **-s**

*An irregular plural noun is a plural noun that does not end in **-s**: *children, men, people, women*. See Chart 4-1.

4-8 POSSESSIVE PRONOUNS AND ADJECTIVES

This pen belongs to me. (a) It's **mine**. (b) It is **my** pen.	(a) and (b) have the same meaning; they both show possession. "Mine" is a possessive pronoun; "my" is a possessive adjective.

POSSESSIVE PRONOUNS	POSSESSIVE ADJECTIVES	
(c) I have **mine**.	I have **my** pen.	A **possessive pronoun** is used alone, without a noun following it.
(d) You have **yours**.	You have **your** pen.	
(e) She has **hers**.	She has **her** pen.	A **possessive adjective** is used only with a noun following it.
(f) He has **his**.	He has **his** pen.	
(g) We have **ours**.	We have **our** pens.	In (j): the possessive **its** is used only with a noun following it. Note that possessive **its** has no apostrophe.*
(h) You have **yours**.	You have **your** pens.	
(i) They have **theirs**.	They have **their** pens.	
(j) _____	I have a book. **Its** cover is black.	

*__its__ = possessive adjective
it's = *it is* (or *it has* when used in the present perfect)

4-9 *A FRIEND OF* + POSSESSIVE

(a) Do you know Greg Smith? He is *a friend of mine*.* (b) We ate dinner with *a friend of Bill's*. INCORRECT: *a friend of Bill*	*A friend of* + *a possessive noun/pronoun* is a special or idomatic expression. It is used to identify another person as one friend among many friends. In (a): *a friend of mine* = one of my friends, but not my only friend. In (b): *a friend of Bill's* = one of Bill's friends; Bill has other friends. In (d): The expression can also be used in the plural.
(c) The Smiths are *friends of mine*.	

*He is my friend may give the idea that the speaker has only one friend. A speaker would normally say *He is one of my friends* or *He is a friend of mine*.

4-10 REFLEXIVE PRONOUNS

myself *yourself* *herself* *himself* *itself* *ourselves* *yourselves* *themselves*	(a) *I saw **myself** in the mirror.* (b) *You* (one person) saw ***yourself**.* (c) *She saw **herself**.* (d) *He saw **himself**.* (e) *It* (e.g, the kitten) *saw **itself**.* (f) *We saw **ourselves**.* (g) *You* (plural) *saw **yourselves**.* (h) *They saw **themselves**.*	Reflexive pronouns end in *-self/-selves*. They are used when the subject (e.g., *I*) and the object (e.g., *myself*) are the same person. The action of the verb is pointed back to the subject of the sentence. INCORRECT: *I saw me in the mirror.*
(i) Greg lives *by himself*. (j) I sat *by myself* on the park bench.	*By* + *a reflexive pronoun* = alone. In (i): Greg lives alone, without family or roommates.	
(k) I *enjoyed myself* at the fair.	*Enjoy* and a few other verbs are commonly followed by a reflexive prounoun. See the list below.	

VERBS AND PHRASES COMMONLY FOLLOWED BY A REFLEXIVE PRONOUN

believe in yourself *blame yourself* *cut yourself* *enjoy yourself* *feel sorry for yourself* *help yourself*	*hurt yourself* *give yourself (something)* *introduce yourself* *kill yourself* *pinch yourself* *be proud of yourself*	*take care of yourself* *talk to yourself* *teach yourself* *tell yourself* *work for yourself* *wish yourself (luck)*

4-11 SINGULAR FORMS OF *OTHER: ANOTHER* vs. *THE OTHER*

ANOTHER

(a) There is a large bowl of apples on the table. Paul is going to eat one apple. If he is still hungry after that, he can eat **another** apple. There are many apples to choose from.	**Another** means "one more out of a group of similar items, one in addition to the one(s) I've already talked about." **Another** is a combination of *an* + *other*, written as one word.

THE OTHER

(b) There are two apples on the table. Paul is going to eat one of them. Sara is going to eat **the other** apple.	**The other** means "the last one in a specific group, the only one that remains from a given number of similar items."
(c) Paul ate one apple. Then he ate **another** apple. (d) Paul ate one apple. Then he ate **another** one. (e) Paul ate one apple. Then he ate **another**.	**Another** and **the other** can be used as an adjective in front of a noun (e.g., *apple*) or in front of the word *one*.
(f) Paul ate one apple. Sara ate **the other** apple. (g) Paul ate one apple. Sara ate **the other** one. (h) Paul ate one apple. Sara ate **the other**.	**Another** and **the other** can also be used alone as a pronoun, as in (e) and (h).

4-12 PLURAL FORMS OF *OTHER: OTHER(S)* vs. *THE OTHER(S)*

OTHER(S)

There are many apples in Paul's kitchen. Paul is holding one apple.
 	
(a) There are ***other*** *apples* in a bowl.
       (adjective + noun)
 	
(b) There are ***other*** *ones* on a plate.
       (adjective + ones)
 	
(c) There are ***others*** on a chair.
       (pronoun)
	Other(*s*) (without ***the***) means "several more out of a group of similar items, several in addition to the one(s) I've already talked about."
	The adjective ***other*** (without an ***-s***) can be used with a plural noun (e.g., *apples*) or with the word *ones*.
	Others (with an ***-s***) is a plural **pronoun**; it is not used with a noun.
	In (c): ***others*** = ***other apples***.

THE OTHER(S)

There are four apples on the table. Paul is going to take one of them.
 	
(d) Sara is going to take ***the other*** *apples*.
       (adjective + noun)
 	
(e) She is going to take ***the other*** *ones*.
       (adjective + ones)
 	
(f) She is going to take ***the others***.
       (pronoun)
	The other(*s*) means "the last ones in a specific group, the remains from a given number of similar items."
	The other (without an ***-s***) can be used as an adjective in front of a noun or the word *ones*, as in (d) and (e).
	The others (with an ***-s***) is a plural **pronoun**; it is not used with a noun.
	In (f): ***the others*** = ***the other apples***.

4-13 SUMMARY OF FORMS OF *OTHER*

	ADJECTIVE	PRONOUN	
SINGULAR	another apple	another	Notice that the word **others** (*other* + final -*s*) is used only as a plural pronoun.
PLURAL	other apples	others	
SINGULAR	the other apple	the other	
PLURAL	the other apples	the others	

EAGLE   CROW   CHICKEN   CHICKEN

There are four birds in the picture.

ADJECTIVES:
The eagle is one bird.
The crow is **another** bird.
The chickens are **the other** birds.

PRONOUNS:
The eagle is one.
The crow is **another.**
The chickens are **the others.**

CAPITALIZE:		
1. The first word of a sentence	(a) **W**e saw a movie last night. **I**t was very good.	*Capitalize* = use a big letter, not a small letter.
2. The names of people	(b) I met **G**eorge **A**dams yesterday.	
3. Titles used with the names of people	(c) I saw **D**octor (**D**r.) Smith. Do you know **P**rofessor (**P**rof.) Alston?	COMPARE: I saw a **d**octor. I saw **D**octor Wilson.
4. Months, days, holidays	(d) I was born in **A**pril. Bob arrived last **M**onday. It snowed on **T**hanksgiving **D**ay.	NOTE: Seasons are not capitalized: *spring, summer, fall/autumn, winter*
5. The names of places: city state/province country continent	(e) He lives in **C**hicago. She was born in **C**alifornia. They are from **M**exico. Tibet is in **A**sia.	COMPARE: She lives in a **c**ity. She lives in New York **C**ity.
ocean lake river desert mountain	They crossed the **A**tlantic **O**cean. Chicago is on **L**ake **M**ichigan. The **N**ile **R**iver flows north. The **S**ahara **D**esert is in Africa. We visited the **R**ocky **M**ountains.	COMPARE: They crossed a **r**iver. They crossed the Yellow **R**iver.
school business	I go to the **U**niversity of **F**lorida. I work for the **G**eneral **E**lectric **C**ompany.	COMPARE: I go to a **u**niversity. I go to the **U**niversity of Texas.
street, etc. building park, zoo	He lives on **G**rand **A**venue. We have class in **R**itter **H**all. I went jogging in **F**orest **P**ark.	COMPARE: We went to a **p**ark. We went to Central **P**ark.
6. The names of courses	(f) I'm taking **C**hemistry 101 this term.	COMPARE: I'm reading a book about **p**sychology. I'm taking **P**sychology 101 this term.
7. The names of languages and nationalities	(g) She speaks **S**panish. We discussed **J**apanese customs.	Words that refer to the names of nations, nationalities and languages are always capitalized.
8. The names of religions	(h) **B**uddism, **C**hristianity, **H**induism, **I**slam, and **J**udaism are major religions in the world. Talal is a **M**oslem.	Words that refer to the names of religions are always capitalized.
9. The pronoun "I."	(i) Yesterday **I** fell off my bicycle.	The pronoun "I" is always capitalized.

CHAPTER **5**

Modal Auxiliaries

5-1 THE FORM OF MODAL AUXILIARIES

The verbs in the list below are called *modal auxiliaries*. They are helping verbs that express a wide range of meanings (ability, permission, possibility, necessity, etc.). Most of the modals have more than one meaning.

AUXILIARY + THE SIMPLE FORM OF A VERB	
can	(a) I *can speak* English.
could	(b) He *couldn't come* to class.
may	(c) It *may rain* tomorrow.
might	(d) It *might rain* tomorrow.
should	(e) Mary *should study* harder.
had better	(f) I *had better study* tonight.
must	(g) Joe *must see* a doctor today.
will	(h) I *will be* in class tomorrow.
would	(i) *Would* you please *close* the door?

Can, *could*, *may*, *might*, *should*, *had better*, *must*, *will*, and *would* are followed by the simple form of a verb.

They are not followed by *to*:
    CORRECT: *I can speak English.*
    INCORRECT: *I can to speak English.*

The main verb never has a final *-s*.
    CORRECT: *Olga can speak English.*
    INCORRECT: *Olga can speaks English.*

AUXILIARY + *TO* + THE SIMPLE FORM OF A VERB	
have to	(j) I *have to study* tonight.
have got to	(k) I *have got to study* tonight.
ought to	(l) Kate *ought to study* harder.

Have, *have got*, and *ought* are followed by an infinitive (*to* + *the simple form of a verb*).

5-2 EXPRESSING ABILITY: *CAN* AND *COULD*

(a) Bob **can play** the piano.* (b) You **can buy** a screwdriver at a hardware store.	**Can** expresses *ability* in the present or future.
(c) I $\left\{ \begin{array}{l} \textit{can't} \\ \textit{cannot} \\ \textit{can not} \end{array} \right\}$ understand that sentence.	The negative form of **can** may be written: **can't**, **cannot**, or **can not**.
(d) Our son **could talk** when he was two years old.	The past form of **can** is **could**.
(e) They $\left\{ \begin{array}{l} \textit{couldn't} \\ \textit{could not} \end{array} \right\}$ come to class yesterday.	The negative of **could**: **couldn't** or **could not**.

*Notice: CORRECT: *Bob can play the piano.*
              INCORRECT: *Bob can to play the piano.*
              INCORRECT: *Bob can plays the piano.*

5-3 EXPRESSING POSSIBILITY: *MAY* AND *MIGHT*
 EXPRESSING PERMISSION: *MAY* AND *CAN*

(a) It **may rain** tomorrow. (b) It **might rain** tomorrow. (c) A: Why isn't John in class? B: I don't know. He $\left\{ \begin{array}{l} \textit{may} \\ \textit{might} \end{array} \right\}$ be sick today.	**May** and **might** express *possibility* in the present or future. They have the same meaning. There is no difference in meaning between (a) and (b).
(d) It **may not rain** tomorrow. (e) It **might not rain** tomorrow.	Negative: **may not** and **might not**. (Do not contract **may** and **might** with **not**.)
(f) **Maybe** it will rain tomorrow. (g) **Maybe** John is sick. (h) John **may be** sick.	**Maybe** (spelled as one word) is an adverb meaning "perhaps." Notice (f) and (g). **May be** (spelled as two words) is a verb form, as in (h): the auxiliary **may** + the main verb **be**.
(i) Yes, children, you **may have** a cookie after dinner. (j) Okay, kids, you **can have** a cookie after dinner.	**May** is also used to give *permission*. Often **can** is used to give *permission*, too. (i) and (j) have the same meaning, but **may** is more formal than **can**.
(k) You **may not** have a cookie. You **can't have** a cookie.	**May not** and **cannot** (**can't**) are used to deny permission (i.e., to say "no").

5-4 USING *COULD* TO EXPRESS POSSIBILITY

(a) A: Why isn't Greg in class? B: I don't know. He **could be** sick. (b) Look at those dark clouds. It **could start** raining any minute.	**Could** can mean *past ability* (see Chart 5-2). But that is not its only meaning. Another meaning of **could** is *possibility*. In (a): "He *could* be sick" has the same meaning as "He *may/might* be sick," i.e., "It is possible that he is sick." In (a), **could** expresses a **present** possibility. In (b), **could** expresses a **future** possibility.

What are their occupations?

The woman **could be** an office manager. She **might be** a teacher. She **may be** a businesswoman.

The man **could be** a businessman. He **might be** a lawyer. He **may be** a teacher.

5-5 ASKING FOR PERMISSION: *MAY I, COULD I, CAN I*

POLITE QUESTION	POSSIBLE ANSWERS	
(a) *May I* please borrow your pen? (b) *Could I* please borrow your pen? (c) *Can I* please borrow your pen?	Yes. Yes. Of course. Yes. Certainly. Of course. Certainly.	People use *may I*, *could I*,* and *can I* to ask polite questions. The questions ask for someone's permission. (a), (b), and (c) have basically the same meaning. Note: *can I* is less formal than *may I* and *could I*.
	Sure. (*informal*) Okay. (*informal*) Uh-huh. (*meaning "yes"*)	*Please* can come at the end of the question: *May I borrow your pen, please?* *Please* can be omitted from the question: *May I borrow your pen?*

*In a polite question, *could* is NOT the past form of *can*.

5-6 ASKING FOR ASSISTANCE:
 WOULD YOU, COULD YOU, WILL YOU, CAN YOU

POLITE QUESTION	POSSIBLE ANSWERS*	
(a) *Would you* please open the door? (b) *Could you* please open the door? (c) *Will you* please open the door? (d) *Can you* please open the door?	Yes. Yes. Of course. Yes. Certainly. Of course. Certainly. I'd be happy to. I'd be glad to. Of course. I'd be happy/glad to. Certainly. I'd be happy/glad to. Sure. (*informal*) Okay. (*informal*) My pleasure. (*informal*) Uh-huh. (*meaning "yes"*)	People use *would you*, *could you*, *will you*, and *can you* to ask polite questions. The questions ask for someone's help or cooperation. (a), (b), (c), and (d) have basically the same meaning. The use of *can*, as in (d), is less formal than the others. NOTE: *May* is NOT used when *you* is the subject of a polite question. INCORRECT: *May you please open the door?*

*Answers to polite questions are usually affirmative. Examples of possible polite negative responses follow:
  I'm sorry, but (I can't, I don't have enough time, my arms are full, etc.).
  I'd like to, but (I can't, I don't have enough time, my arms are full, etc.).

5-7 EXPRESSING ADVICE: SHOULD, OUGHT TO, HAD BETTER

(a) My clothes are dirty. I { **should** / **ought to** / **had better** } *wash* them.	**Should**, **ought to**, and **had better** have basically the same meaning. They mean: "*This is a good idea. This is good advice.*"
(b) You need your sleep. You **shouldn't** stay up late.	Negative: **should** + **not** = **shouldn't**.*
(c) **I'd** better / **You'd** better / **He'd** better / **She'd** better / **We'd** better / **They'd** better } study tonight.	Contraction of **had** = **'d**. NOTE: Usually **had** is the past form of **have**. However, in the expression **had better**, **had** is used as part of an idiom and the meaning is not past. The meaning is present or future.

*__Ought to__ is usually not used in the negative.
The negative of **had better** is **had better not**, and it often carries a warning of bad consequences.
   You had better not be late! If you are late, you will get into a lot of trouble.

5-8 EXPRESSING NECESSITY: HAVE TO, HAVE GOT TO, MUST

(a) I have a very important test tomorrow. I { **have to** / **have got to** / **must** } *study* tonight.	**Have to**, **have got to**, and **must** have basically the same meaning. They express the idea that something is *necessary*.
	Have to is used much more frequently than **must** in everyday speech and writing.* **Have got to** is generally used only in informal speech and writing.
(b) I **have to** ("hafta") *go* downtown today. (c) Rita **has to** ("hasta") *go* to the bank. (d) I've **got to** ("gotta") *study* tonight.	Usual pronunciation: **have to** = "hafta" **has to** = "hasta" (**have**) **got to** = "gotta"
(e) I **had to** *study* last night.	The past form of **have to**, **have got to**, and **must** (meaning necessity) is **had to**.

*__Must__ means that something is **very** necessary; there is no other choice. **Must** is used much less frequently than **have to** in everyday speech and writing. **Must** is a "strong" word.

5-9 EXPRESSING LACK OF NECESSITY: *DO NOT HAVE TO* EXPRESSING PROHIBITION: *MUST NOT*

(a) I finished all of my homework this afternoon. I **don't have to study** tonight. (b) Tomorrow is a holiday. Mary **doesn't have to go** to class.	***Don't/doesn't have to*** expresses the idea that something is *not necessary*.
(c) Children, you **must not play** with matches! (d) We **must not use** that door. The sign says: PRIVATE: DO NOT ENTER.	***Must not*** expresses *prohibition*. (DO NOT DO THIS!)
(e) You **mustn't play** with matches.	***Must*** + ***not*** = ***mustn't***. (Note: The first "t" is not pronounced.)

If you are in a canoe, you **must not stand** up and walk around. If you do, the canoe will probably tip over.

5-10 MAKING LOGICAL CONCLUSIONS: *MUST*

(a) A: Nancy is yawning. B: She **must be** sleepy.	In (a): SPEAKER B is making a logical guess. He bases his guess on the information that Nancy is yawning. His logical conclusion, his "best guess," is that Nancy is sleepy. He uses **must** to express his logical conclusion.

(b) LOGICAL CONCLUSION: Amy plays tennis every day. She **must like** to play tennis.
 (c) NECESSITY: If you want to get into the movie theater, you **must buy** a ticket.
	COMPARE: **Must** can express:
	   • a logical conclusion, as in (b).
	   • necessity, as in (c).

(d) NEGATIVE LOGICAL CONCLUSION: Eric ate everything on his plate except the pickle. He **must not like** pickles.
 (e) PROHIBITION: There are sharks in the ocean near our hotel. We **must not go** swimming there.
	COMPARE: **Must not** can express:
	   • a negative logical conclusion, as in (d).
	   • prohibition, as in (e).

5-11 GIVING INSTRUCTIONS: IMPERATIVE SENTENCES

COMMAND
  (a) *General:* **Open** the door!
       Soldier: Yes, sir!
REQUEST
  (b) *Teacher:* **Open** the door, please.
      Student: Okay, I'd be happy to.
DIRECTIONS
  (c) *Barbara:* Could you tell me how to get to the post office?
    Stranger: Certainly. **Walk** two blocks down this street. **Turn** left and **walk** three more blocks. It's on the right hand side of the street.
	Imperative sentences are used to give commands, make polite requests, and give directions.
	The difference between a command and a request lies in the speaker's tone of voice and the use of **please**.
	Please can come at the beginning or end of a request:
	    Open the door, please.
	    Please open the door.

(d) **Close** the window.
  (e) Please **sit** down.
  (f) **Be** quiet!
  (g) **Don't walk** on the grass.
  (h) Please **don't wait** for me.
  (i) **Don't be** late.
	The simple form of a verb is used in imperative sentences. The understood subject of the sentence is **you** (meaning the person the speaker is talking to): (*You*) *close the window.*
	Negative form:
	    Don't + *the simple form of a verb.*

DON'T CROSS THIS FIELD UNLESS YOU CAN DO IT IN 9.9 SECONDS. THE BULL CAN DO IT IN 10. (NO TRESPASSING)

5-12 MAKING SUGGESTIONS: *LET'S* AND *WHY DON'T*

(a) A: It's hot today. **Let's go** to the beach. B: Okay. Good idea. (b) A: It's hot today. **Why don't we go** to the beach? B: Okay. Good idea.	**Let's** (*do something*) and **why don't we** (*do something*) have the same meaning. They are used to make suggestions about activities for you and me. **Let's** = *let us*.
(c) A: I'm tired. B: **Why don't you take** a nap? A: That's a good idea. I think I will.	People use **why don't you** (*do something*) to make a friendly suggestion, to give friendly advice.

5-13 STATING PREFERENCES: *PREFER, LIKE...BETTER, WOULD RATHER*

(a) I **prefer** apples **to** oranges. (b) I **prefer** *watching* TV **to** *studying*.	*prefer* + NOUN + *to* + NOUN *prefer* + -ING VERB + *to* + -ING VERB
(c) I **like** apples **better than** oranges. (d) I **like** *watching* TV **better than** *studying*.	*like* + NOUN + *better than* + NOUN *like* + -ING VERB + *better than* + -ING VERB
(e) Ann **would rather have** an apple **than** (**have**) an orange. (f) **I'd rather visit** a big city **than live** there.	In (e) and (f): **would rather** and **than** are followed immediately by the simple form of a verb (e.g., *have, visit, live*).*
(g) **I'd/You'd/She'd/He'd/We'd/They'd** rather have an apple.	Contraction of **would** = **'d**.
(h) **Would you rather** have an apple **or** an orange?	In (h): In a polite question, **would rather** can be followed by **or** to offer someone a choice.

*INCORRECT: *Ann would rather has an apple.*
INCORRECT: *I'd rather visit a big city than to live there.*
INCORRECT: *I'd rather visit a big city than living there.*

CHAPTER **6**

Asking Questions

6-1 YES/NO QUESTIONS AND SHORT ANSWERS

YES/NO QUESTIONS	SHORT ANSWER (+ LONG ANSWER)	A *yes/no question* is a question that can be answered by "yes" or "no" (or their equivalents, such as "yeah" or "nah," and "uh huh" or "huh uh").
(a) **Do you know** Jim Smith?	**Yes, I do**. (I know Jim Smith.) **No, I don't**. (I don't know Jim Smith.)	
(b) **Did it rain** last night?	**Yes, it did**. (It rained last night.) **No, it didn't**. (It didn't rain last night.)	
(c) **Are you studying** English?	**Yes, I am**.★ (I'm studying English.) **No, I'm not**. (I'm not studying English.)	
(d) **Was Ann** in class?	**Yes, she was**. (Ann was in class.) **No, she wasn't**. (Ann wasn't in class.)	
(e) **Will Rob be** here soon?	**Yes, he will**.★ (Rob will be here soon.) **No, he won't**. (Rob won't be here soon.)	
(f) **Can you swim**?	**Yes, I can**. (I can swim.) **No, I can't**. (I can't swim.)	

★NOTE: In an affirmative answer (*yes*), a helping verb is not contracted with the subject.
    In (c): CORRECT: *Yes, I am.* (The spoken emphasis is on **am**.)
            INCORRECT: *Yes, I'm.*
    In (e): CORRECT: *Yes, he will.* (The spoken emphasis is on **will**.)
            INCORRECT: *Yes, he'll.*

6-2 YES/NO QUESTIONS AND INFORMATION QUESTIONS

A yes/no question = a question that may be answered by "yes" or "no."

A: Does Ann live in Montreal?
B: Yes, she does. OR: No, she doesn't.

An information question = a question that asks for information by using a question word: ***where, when, why, who, whom, what, which, whose, how.***

A: Where does Ann live?
B: In Montreal.

(QUESTION WORD)	HELPING VERB	SUBJECT	MAIN VERB	(REST OF SENTENCE)	
(a)	***Does***	*Ann*	***live***	in Montreal?	The same subject-verb word order is used in both yes/no and information questions:
(b) Where	*does*	*Ann*	***live?***		HELPING VERB + SUBJECT + MAIN VERB
(c)	***Is***	*Sara*	***studying***	at the library?	
(d) Where	*is*	*Sara*	***studying?***		
(e)	***Will***	*you*	***graduate***	next year?	
(f) When	***will***	*you*	***graduate?***		
(g)	***Did***	*they*	***see***	Jack?	In (i) and (j): Main verb ***be*** in simple present and simple past (***am, is, are, was, were***) precedes the subject. It has the same position as a helping verb.
(h) Who(m)*	***did***	*they*	***see?***		
(i)	***Is***	*Heidi*		at home?	
(j) Where	*is*	*Heidi?*			
(k)		*Who*	***came***	to dinner?	When the question word (e.g., ***who*** or ***what***) is the subject of the question, the usual question word order is not used. No form of ***do*** is used. Notice (k) and (l).
(l)		*What*	***happened***	yesterday?	

*See Chart 6-3 for a discussion of ***who(m)***.

Do frogs **eat** insects?
What **do** frogs **eat**?

6-3 USING *WHO*, *WHO(M)*, AND *WHAT*

QUESTION	ANSWER	

s
(a) **Who** came?
	s
	Someone came.
		In (a): **Who** is used as the subject (**s**) of a question.
		In (b): **Who(m)** is used as the object (**o**) in a question.
		Whom is used in formal English. In everyday spoken English, **who** is usually used instead of **whom**:
		  FORMAL: *Whom did you see?*
		  INFORMAL: *Who did you see?*

o **s** (b) **Who(m)** did you see?	**s** **o** I saw **someone**.	

s
(c) **What** happened?
	s
	Something happened.
		What can be used as either the subject or the object in a question.
		Notice in (a) and (c): When **who** or **what** is used as the subject of a question, usual question word order is not used; no form of **do** is used.
		  CORRECT: *Who came?*
		  INCORRECT: *Who did come?*

o **s** (d) **What** did you see?	**s** **o** I saw **something**.	

WHO

Who saw an accident? Mary.
Mary saw an accident.

WHAT

What did Mary see? An accident.
Mary saw an accident.

6-4 USING *WHAT* + A FORM OF *DO*

What + *a form of* **do** is used to ask questions about activities.
(Examples of forms of **do:** *am doing, will do, are going to do, did,* etc.)

QUESTION	ANSWER
(a) *What* **does** Bob **do** every morning? ⟶	He *goes to class.*
(b) *What* **did** you **do** yesterday? ⟶	I *went downtown.*
(c) *What* **is** your roommate **doing**? ⟶	She's *studying.*
(d) *What* **are** you **going to do** tomorrow? ⟶	I'm *going to go to the beach.*
(e) *What* **do** you **want to do** tonight? ⟶	I *want to go to a movie.*
(f) *What* **would** you **like to do** tomorrow? ⟶	I *would like to visit Jim.*
(g) *What* **will** you **do** tomorrow? ⟶	I'll *go downtown.*
(h) *What* **should** I **do** about my headache? ⟶	You *should take an aspirin.*

What **does** a bear **do** in the winter?
It hibernates.

6-5   USING *WHAT KIND OF*

QUESTION	ANSWER	

(a) **What kind of** *shoes* did you buy? ⟶	Boots.
	Sandals.
	Tennis shoes.
	Loafers.
	Running shoes.
	High heels.
	(etc.)
		What kind of asks for information about a specific type (a specific kind) in a general category.
		
		In (a):
		general category = shoes
		specific kinds = boots
		  sandals,
		  tennis shoes,
		  etc.

(b) **What kind of** *fruit* do you like best? ⟶	Apples. Bananas. Oranges. Grapefruit. Grapes. Strawberries. (etc.)	

6-6   USING *WHICH*

(a) *Tom:* May I borrow a pen from you? *Ann:* Sure. I have two pens. This pen has black ink. That pen has red ink. **Which (pen/one) do you want**? *Tom:* That one. Thanks. (b) **Which pen** do you want? (c) **Which one** do you want? (d) **Which** do you want?	In (a): Ann uses **which** (not *what*) because she wants Tom to choose. **Which** is used when the speaker wants someone to make a choice, when the speaker is offering alternatives: *this one or that one; these or those.* (b), (c), and (d) have the same meaning.
(e) *Sue:* I like these earrings, and I like those earrings. *Bob:* **Which (earrings/ones) are you going to buy?** *Sue:* I think I'll get these. (f) **Which earrings** are you going to buy? (g) **Which ones** are you going to buy? (h) **Which** are you going to buy?	**Which** can be used with either singular or plural nouns. (f), (g), and (h) have the same meaning.

6-7 USING *WHOSE*

QUESTION	ANSWER	
(a) **Whose** (**book**) is this?	It's John's (book).	**Whose** asks about possession. Notice in (a): the speaker of the question may omit the noun (*book*) if the meaning is clear to the listener.
(b) **Whose** (**books**) are those?	They're mine (OR: my books).	
(c) **Whose car** did you borrow?	I borrowed Karen's (car).	
COMPARE:		**Who's** and **whose** have the same pronunciation.
(d) **Who's** that?	Mary Smith.	**Who's** = a contraction of **who is**.
(e) **Whose** is that?	Mary's.	**Whose** = asks about possession.*

*See Charts 4-7 and 4-8 for ways of expressing possession.

SUSAN

Who is this? Susan.
(This is Susan.)

Whose basketball is this? Susan's.
(It's Susan's basketball.)

Whose clothes are those? Susan's.
(They're Susan's clothes.)

ERIC

Who is that? Eric.
(That is Eric.)

Whose notebook is that? Eric's.
(It's Eric's notebook.)

6-8 USING *HOW*

QUESTION	ANSWER	
(a) *How* did you get here? ⟶	{ I drove./By car. I took a taxi./By taxi. I took a bus./By bus. I flew./By plane. I took a train./By train. I walked./On foot.	*How* has many uses. One use of *how* is to ask about means (ways) of transportation.
(b) *How old* are you? ⟶ (c) *How tall* is he? ⟶ (d) *How big* is your apartment? ⟶ (e) *How sleepy* are you? ⟶ (f) *How hungry* are you? ⟶ (g) *How soon* will you be ready? ⟶ (h) *How well* does he speak English? ➤ (i) *How quickly* can you get here? ⟶	Twenty-one. About six feet. It has three rooms. Very sleepy. I'm starving. In five minutes. Very well. I can get there in 30 minutes.	*How* is often used with adjectives (e.g., *old*, *big*) and adverbs (e.g., *well*, *quickly*).

6-9 USING *HOW OFTEN*

QUESTION	ANSWER	
(a) *How often* do you go shopping?	{ Every day. Once a week. About twice a week. Every other day or so.★ Three times a month.	*How often* asks about frequency.
(b) *How many times a day* do you eat? *How many times a week* do you go shopping? *How many times a month* do you go to the bank? *How many times a year* do you take a vacation?	Three or four. Two. Once. Once or twice.	Other ways of asking *how often*: *how many times* { *a day* *a week* *a month* *a year*

★*Every other day* means Monday yes, Tuesday no, Wednesday yes, Thursday no, etc. *Or so* means *approximately.*

6-10 USING *HOW FAR*

(a) *It is* 289 miles *from* St. Louis *to* Chicago.** (b) *It is* 289 miles $\begin{cases} \textit{from} \text{ St. Louis } \textit{to} \text{ Chicago.} \\ \textit{from} \text{ Chicago } \textit{to} \text{ St. Louis.} \\ \textit{to} \text{ Chicago } \textit{from} \text{ St. Louis.} \\ \textit{to} \text{ St. Louis } \textit{from} \text{ Chicago.} \end{cases}$	The most common way of expressing distance: *It is* + *distance* + *from/to* + *to/from*. In (b): All four expressions with *from* and *to* have the same meaning.

(c) A: *How far is it* from St. Louis to Chicago?
    B: 289 miles.
 (d) A: *How far do you* live from school?
    B: Four blocks.
	How far is used to ask questions about distance.

(e) *How many miles* is it from St. Louis to Chicago?
 (f) *How many kilometers* is it to Montreal from here?
 (g) *How many blocks* is it to the post office?
	Other ways to ask *how far*:
	    how many miles
	    how many kilometers
	    how many blocks

**1 mile = 1.609 kilometers.
  1 kilometer = 0.614 mile.

6-11 EXPRESSING LENGTH OF TIME: *IT* + *TAKE*

IT + *TAKE* + (SOMEONE) + TIME EXPRESSION + INFINITIVE*				
(a) *It*	takes		*six hours*	*to drive*	to Chicago from here.
(b) *It*	took	Janet	*a long time*	*to finish*	her composition.

*An infinitive = *to* + *the simple form of a verb.* See Chart 10-1.

6-12 USING *HOW LONG*

QUESTION	ANSWER	
(a) *How long does it take* to drive to Chicago from here?	Two days.	*How long* asks for information about length of time.
(b) *How long* did you study last night?	Four hours.	
(c) *How long* will you be in Florida?	Ten days.	
(d) *How many days* will you be in Florida?	Ten.	Other ways of asking *how long*: *how many* + $\begin{cases} \textit{minutes} \\ \textit{hours} \\ \textit{days} \\ \textit{weeks} \\ \textit{months} \\ \textit{years} \end{cases}$

6-13 MORE QUESTIONS WITH *HOW*

QUESTION	ANSWER	
(a) ***How do you spell*** "coming"?	C-O-M-I-N-G.	To answer (a): Spell the word.
(b) ***How do you say*** "yes" in Japanese?	*Hai.*	To answer (b): Say the word.
(c) ***How do you say/pronounce*** this word?	_____	To answer (c): Pronounce the word.
(d) ***How are you getting along?***	Great.	In (d), (e), and (f): How is your life? Is your life okay? Do you have any problems?
(e) ***How are you doing?***	Fine.	NOTE: (f) is often used in greetings:
(f) ***How's it going?***	Okay. So-so.	*Hi, Bob. How's it going?*
(g) ***How do you feel?*** ***How are you feeling?***	Terrific! Wonderful! Great! Fine. Okay. So-so. A bit under the weather. Not so good. Terrible! Lousy. Awful!	The questions in (g) ask about health or about general emotional state.
(h) ***How do you do?***	How do you do?	***How do you do?*** is used by both speakers when they are introduced to each other in a somewhat formal situation.*

*A: *Dr. Erickson, I'd like to introduce you to a friend of mine, Dick Brown. Dick, this is my biology professor, Dr. Erickson.*
  B: ***How do you do**, Mr. Brown?*
  C: ***How do you do**, Dr. Erickson? I'm pleased to meet you.*

How did Billy break Jason's bike?
He ran into a brick wall.
(Billy broke Jason's bike by running into a brick wall.)

6-14 USING *HOW ABOUT* AND *WHAT ABOUT*

(a) A: We need one more player.
   B: ***How about (what about)* Jack**? Let's ask him if he wants to play.
(b) A: What time should we meet?
   B: ***How about (what about)* three o'clock?**
	How about and *what about* have the same meaning and usage. They are used to make suggestions or offers.
	
	How about and *what about* are followed by a noun (or pronoun) or the *-ing* form of a verb.

(c) A: What should we do this afternoon?
   B: ***How about* going** to the zoo?
(d) A: ***What about* asking** Sally over for dinner?
   B: Okay. Good idea.
	Note: *How about* and *what about* are used in informal spoken English frequently, but are usually not used in writing.

(e) A: I'm tired. ***How about you?***
   B: Yes, I'm tired too.
(f) A: Are you hungry?
   B: No. ***What about you?***
   A: I'm a little hungry.
	How about you? and *What about you?* are used to ask a question that refers to the information or question that immediately preceded. In (e): *How about you? = Are you tired?* In (f): *What about you? = Are you hungry?*

6-15 TAG QUESTIONS

AFFIRMATIVE	**NEGATIVE**	A tag question is a question that is added onto the end of a sentence. An auxiliary verb is used in a tag question.
(a) *You **know** Bob Wilson,*	***don't** you?*	
(b) *Mary **is** from Chicago,*	***isn't** she?*	In (a), (b), and (c): When the main verb is affirmative, the tag question is negative.
(c) *Jerry **can play** the piano,*	***can't** he?*	
NEGATIVE	**AFFIRMATIVE**	In (c), (d), and (e): When the main verb is negative, the tag question is affirmative.
(d) *You **don't know** Jack Smith,*	***do** you?*	
(e) *Mary **isn't** from New York,*	***is** she?*	
(f) *Jerry **can't speak** Arabic,*	***can** he?*	

Notice in the following: I (the speaker) use a tag question because I expect you (the listener) to agree with me. I give my idea while asking a question at the same time.*

THE SPEAKER'S IDEA	THE SPEAKER'S QUESTION	EXPECTED ANSWER
(g) I think that you know Bob Wilson.	You **know** Bob Wilson, **don't** you?	**Yes,** I do.
(h) I think that you don't know Jack Smith.	You **don't know** Jack Smith, **do** you?	**No,** I don't.
(i) I think that Mary is from Chicago.	Mary **is** from Chicago, **isn't** she?	**Yes,** she is.
(j) I think that Mary isn't from New York.	Mary **isn't** from New York, **is** she?	**No,** she isn't.
(k) I think that Jerry can play the piano.	Jerry **can play** the piano, **can't** he?	**Yes,** he can.
(l) I think that Jerry can't speak Arabic.	Jerry **can't speak** Arabic, **can** he?	**No,** he can't.

*COMPARE: ***A yes/no question:***
   A: Do you know Bob Wilson? *(The speaker has no idea. The speaker is simply looking for information.)*
   B: Yes, I do. OR: No, I don't.

   A tag question:
   A: You know Bob Wilson, don't you? *(The speaker believes that you know Bob Wilson. The speaker wants to make sure that his/her idea is correct.)*
   B: Yes, I do. *(The speaker expects you to answer **yes**. You can, however, answer **no** if you do not know Bob Wilson.)*

CHAPTER *7*

The Present Perfect and the Past Perfect

7-1 THE PAST PARTICIPLE

	SIMPLE FORM	SIMPLE PAST	**PAST PARTICIPLE**	
				The **past participle** is one of the principal parts of a verb. (See Chart 2-3.)
REGULAR VERBS	finish stop wait	finished stopped waited	**finished** **stopped** **waited**	The past participle is used in the PRESENT PERFECT tense and the PAST PERFECT tense.*
IRREGULAR VERBS	see make put	saw made put	**seen** **made** **put**	The past participle of regular verbs is the same as the simple past form: both end in *-ed*. See Chart 2-4 for a list of irregular verbs.

*The past participle is also used in the passive. See Chapter 11.

I *see* the skeleton of a dinosaur on this page.

When I want to the Museum of Natural History last year, I *saw* the skeleton of dinosaur.

No one has ever seen a live dinosaur. Dinosaurs became extinct 165 million years ago.

STATEMENT: **HAVE/HAS + PAST PARTICIPLE** (a) I **have finished** my work. (b) The students **have finished** Chapter 5. (c) Jim **has eaten** lunch.	The basic form of the present perfect: **have or has** + **the past participle**. Use **have** with *I, you, we, they,* or a plural noun (e.g., *students*). Use **has** with *she, he, it,* or a singular noun (e.g., *Jim*).
(d) **I've/You've/We've/They've** eaten lunch. (e) **She's/He's** eaten lunch. (f) **It's** been cold for the last three days.	With pronouns, **have** is contracted to apostrophe + **ve** ('ve) and **has** to apostrophe + **s** ('s).
NEGATIVE: **HAVE/HAS + NOT + PAST PARTICIPLE** (g) I **have not** (**haven't**) **finished** my work. (h) Ann **has not** (**hasn't**) **eaten** lunch.	*have + not = haven't* *has + not = hasn't*
QUESTION: **HAVE/HAS + SUBJECT + PAST PARTICIPLE** (i) **Have you finished** your work? (j) **Has Jim eaten** lunch? (k) How long **have you lived** here?	In a question, the helping verb (*have* or *has*) precedes the subject.

(l) A: Have you seen that movie?
    B: *Yes, I **have**.* OR: *No, I **haven't**.*
(m) A: Has Jim eaten lunch?
    B: *Yes, he **has**.* OR: *No, he **hasn't**.*
	The helping verb (*have* or *has*) is used in a short answer to a yes/no question.
	The helping verb in the short answer is not contracted with the pronoun.

Jim **has** already **eaten** lunch.   Ann **hasn't eaten** lunch yet.

7-3 MEANINGS OF THE PRESENT PERFECT

(time?) graph	(a) Jim **has** already **eaten** lunch. (b) Ann **hasn't eaten** lunch yet. (c) **Have** you ever **eaten** at that restaurant? (d) I**'ve** never **eaten** there.	The present perfect expresses activities or situations that occurred (or did not occur) "before now," at some unspecified time in the past.*
graph	(e) Pete **has eaten** at that restaurant many times. (f) I**'ve been** to that theater five or six times. (g) I**'ve had** three tests so far this week.	The present perfect expresses activities that were repeated several or many times in the past. The exact times are unspecified.
graph	(h) Erica **has lived** in this city *since 1989*. (i) I **have known** Ben *for ten years*. (j) We**'ve been** in class *since ten o'clock this morning*.	When the present perfect is used with **since** or **for**, it expresses situations that began in the past and continue to the present.

*If the exact time is specified, the simple past tense is used. (See Chart 7-4.)

  SPECIFIC TIME: Jim **ate** lunch *at 12:00/two hours ago/yesterday.*

  UNSPECIFIED TIME: Jim **has** already **eaten** lunch. (*at some unspecified time before now*)

7-4 USING THE SIMPLE PAST vs. THE PRESENT PERFECT

SIMPLE PAST: (a) I **finished** my work *two hours ago*. PRESENT PERFECT: (b) I **have already*** **finished** my work.	In (a): I finished my work at a specific time in the past (*two hours ago*). In (b): I finished my work at an unspecified time in the past (sometime before now).
SIMPLE PAST: (c) I **was** in Europe *last year/three years ago/in 1989/in 1985 and 1989/when I was ten years old.* PRESENT PERFECT: (d) I **have been** in Europe *many times/several times/a couple of times/once/* (no mention of time).	The simple past expresses an activity that occurred at a specific time (or times) in the past, as in (a) and (c). The present perfect expresses an activity that occurred at an unspecified time (or times) in the past, as in (b) and (d).

*Already has the same usual placement as frequency adverbs. (See Chart 7-8.) *Already* means "before." (See Chart 7-9.)

SINCE		
(a) I *have been* here since eight o'clock. since Tuesday. since May. since 1989. since January 3, 1988. since the beginning of the semester. since yesterday. since last month.		*Since* is followed by the mention of *a specific point in time*: an hour, a day, a month, a year, etc. *Since* expresses the idea that an activity began at a specific time in the past and continues to the present. The present perfect also expresses the idea that an activity began in the past and continues to the present.
(b) INCORRECT: I am living here since May. (c) INCORRECT: I live here since May. INCORRECT: I am here since May. (d) INCORRECT: I lived here since May. INCORRECT: I was here since May. (e) CORRECT: **I *have lived* here *since* May.*** CORRECT: **I *have been* here *since* May.**		The *present perfect* is used in sentences with *since*. In (b): The present progressive is NOT used. In (c): The simple present is NOT used. In (d): The simple past is NOT used.
MAIN CLAUSE (present perfect) (f) I *have lived* here (g) Al *has met* many people	*SINCE* CLAUSE (simple past) since I *was* a child. since he *came* here.	*Since* may also introduce a time clause (i.e., a subject and verb may follow *since*). Notice in the examples: The present perfect is used in the main clause; the simple past is used in the "*since* clause."
FOR		
(h) I *have been* here for ten minutes. for two hours. for five days. for about three weeks. for almost six months. for many years. for a long time.		*For* is followed by the mention of a *length of time*: two minutes, three hours, four days, five weeks, etc. Note: If the noun ends in *-s* (*hours, days, weeks*, etc.), use *for* in the time expression, not *since*.
(i) I *have lived* here *for two years*. I moved here two years ago, and I still live here. (j) I *lived* in Chicago *for two years*. I don't live in Chicago now.		In (i): The use of the present perfect in a sentence with *for* + *a length of time* means that the action began in the past and continues to the present. In (j): The use of the simple past means that the action began and ended in the past.

*ALSO CORRECT: *I have been living* here *since May*. See Chart 7-6 for a discussion of the present perfect progressive.

7-6 THE PRESENT PERFECT PROGRESSIVE

(a) I **have been studying** English at this school since May. (b) Adam **has been sleeping** for two hours.	Form of the present perfect progressive: **have/has + been + ing** The present perfect progressive expresses how long an activity has been in progress.
(c) How long **have you been studying** English here? (d) How long **has** Adam **been sleeping**?	Question form: **have/has + subject + been + -ing**
COMPARE (e) and (f). PRESENT PROGRESSIVE: (e) I **am sitting** in class right now.	The present progressive expresses an activity that is in progress (is happening) right now.
PRESENT PERFECT PROGRESSIVE: (f) I **have been sitting** in class { since 9 o'clock. / for 45 minutes.	The present perfect progressive expresses the duration (the length of time) an activity is in progress. Time expressions with **since** and **for** are used with the present perfect progressive.

Right now Mr. Chapman **is feeding** the pigeons in Grant Park.

He **has been feeding** the pigeons in Grant Park for ten minutes.

7-7 THE PRESENT PERFECT vs. THE PRESENT PERFECT PROGRESSIVE

PRESENT PERFECT: (a) Rita **has talked** to Josh on the phone many times.	The present perfect is used to express repeated actions in the past, as in (a).
PRESENT PERFECT PROGRESSIVE: (b) Rita **has been talking** to Josh on the phone for twenty minutes.	The present perfect progressive is used to express the *duration* of an activity that is in progress, i.e., how long something has continued to the present time. In (b): Their conversation began 20 minutes ago and has continued since that time. It has been in progress for 20 minutes. It is still in progress.
PRESENT PERFECT: (c) I **have lived** here for two years. PRESENT PERFECT PROGRESSIVE: (d) I **have been living** here for two years.	With some verbs (e.g., *live, work, teach*), duration can be expressed by either the present perfect or the present perfect progressive. (c) and (d) have essentially the same meaning.

7-8 MIDSENTENCE ADVERBS

(a) I **always** *get* up at 6:30. (b) You **probably** *know* the right answer.	Some adverbs typically occur in the middle of a sentence, not at the beginning or end of a sentence. These adverbs, such as **always**, are called "midsentence adverbs."

LIST OF COMMON MIDSENTENCE ADVERBS
 	
 FREQUENCY ADVERBS   OTHER MIDSENTENCE ADVERBS
 	
 positive
    ever   **already***
    always   **finally**
    almost always   **just**
    usually*   **probably**
    often*
    frequently*
    generally*
    sometimes*
    occasionally*
 	
 negative
    seldom
    rarely
    hardly ever
    almost never
    never
    not ever
	The adverbs in the list usually occur in the middle of a sentence. When these adverbs occur in the middle of a sentence, they have special positions, as shown in examples (c) through (h) below.
	
	 The adverbs with an asterisk (*) may also occur at the beginning or end of a sentence.
	    I **sometimes** *get up at 6:30.*
	    Sometimes *I get up at 6:30.*
	    I get up at 6:30 **sometimes**.
	
	 The other adverbs in the list (without asterisks) rarely occur at the beginning or end of a sentence. Their usual position is in the middle of a sentence.

(c) He **always** *comes* to class. She **finally** *finished* her work.	In (c): In a STATEMENT, midsentence adverbs come in front of simple present and simple past verbs (except *be*).
(d) They *are* **always** on time for class. He *was* **probably** at home last night.	In (d): Midsentence adverbs follow *be* in the simple present (*am, is, are*) and simple past (*was, were*).

(e) I *will* **always** *remember* her.
      She *is* **probably** *sleeping.*
      They *have* **finally** *finished* their work.
	In (e): Midsentence adverbs come between a helping verb and a main verb.

(f) *Do* **you always** *eat* breakfast?
      Did **Tom finally** *finish* his work?
      Is **she usually** on time for class?
	In (f): In a QUESTION, the adverbs come directly after the subject.

(g) She **usually doesn't** *eat* breakfast. I **probably won't** *go* to the meeting.	In (g): In a NEGATIVE sentence, most adverbs come in front of the negative verb (except *always* and *ever*).
(h) She **doesn't always** *eat* breakfast. He **isn't ever** on time for class.	In (h): **Always** and **ever** follow a negative helping verb or negative *be*.
(i) CORRECT: She never eats meat. (j) INCORRECT: She doesn't never eat meat.	Negative adverbs (*seldom, rarely, hardly ever, never*) are NOT used with a negative verb.

7-9 USING *ALREADY, YET, STILL,* AND *ANYMORE*

ALREADY	(a) The mail came an hour ago. **The mail is *already* here.**	Idea of *already*: Something happened before now, before this time. *Position: midsentence.**
YET	(b) I expected the mail an hour ago, but **it hasn't come *yet*.**	Idea of *yet*: Something did not happen before now (up to this time), but it may happen in the future. *Position: end of sentence.*
STILL	(c) It was cold yesterday. **It is *still* cold today.** (d) I could play the piano when I was a child. **I can *still* play the piano.** (e) The mail didn't come an hour ago. **The mail *still* hasn't come.**	Idea of *still*: A situation continues to exist from past to present without change. *Position: midsentence.**
ANYMORE	(f) I lived in Chicago two years ago, but then I moved to another city. **I don't live in Chicago *anymore*.**	Idea of *anymore*: A past situation does not continue to exist at present; a past situation has changed. ***Anymore*** has the same meaning as *any longer*. *Position: end of sentence.*
NOTE: ***Already*** is used in *affirmative* sentences. ***Yet*** and ***anymore*** are used in *negative* sentences. ***Still*** is used in either *affirmative* or *negative* sentences.		

*See Chart 7-8 for the usual positions of midsentence adverbs.

Bob is on a camping trip. It's 10:00 PM.
Bob is *already* in his tent, but he isn't asleep *yet*.
He is *still* awake because he is uncomfortable.

Bob's wife doesn't go camping with him ***anymore***
because she doesn't like to sleep in a tent.

7-10 USING THE PAST PERFECT

COMPARE (a) THE PRESENT PERFECT AND (b) THE PAST PERFECT:		
PRESENT PERFECT before now · now	(a) I am not hungry now. I **have** already **eaten**.	The present perfect expresses an activity that *occurred "before now," at an unspecified time in the past.*
PAST PERFECT before 1:00 · 1:00 pm	(b) I was not hungry at 1:00 P.M. I **had** already **eaten**.	The past perfect expresses an activity that *occurred before another time in the past.* In (b): I ate at noon. I was not hungry at 1:00 P.M. because I had already eaten before 1:00 P.M.

COMPARE (c) THE PAST PROGRESSIVE AND (d) THE PAST PERFECT:		
PAST PROGRESSIVE began eating · Bob came *eating in progress*	(c) I **was eating** when Bob came.	The past progressive expresses an activity that was *in progress* at a particular time in the past. In (c): I began to eat at noon. Bob came at 12:10. My meal was in progress when Bob came.
PAST PERFECT finished eating · Bob came	(d) I **had eaten** when Bob came.	The past perfect expresses an activity that was *completed before a particular time in the past.* In (d): I ate at noon. Bob came at 1:00 P.M. My meal was completed before Bob came.

CHAPTER 8

Count/Noncount Nouns and Articles

8-1 COUNT AND NONCOUNT NOUNS

	SINGULAR	PLURAL	
COUNT NOUN	*a* chair *one* chair	chairs *two* chairs *three* chairs *some* chairs *several* chairs *a lot of* chairs *many* chairs *a few* chairs	Some nouns are called COUNT NOUNS: (1) In the singular, they can be preceded by *a/an* or *one*. (2) They have a plural form: *-s* or *-es*.*
NONCOUNT NOUN	furniture *some* furniture *a lot of* furniture *much* furniture *a little* furniture	Ø	Some nouns are called NONCOUNT NOUNS: (1) They are NOT immediately preceded by *a/an* or *one*. (2) They do NOT have a plural form (no final *-s* is added).

*See Chart 4-1.

Rita is wearing **two rings** on her left hand.

(a) I bought **some furniture**.
 (b) I got **some mail** yesterday.
	A noncount noun* is NOT preceded by **a/an**, **one**, **two**, **three**, etc.
	     INCORRECT: *I bought a furniture.*
	 A noncount noun does NOT have a plural form.
	     INCORRECT: *I bought some furnitures.*

INDIVIDUAL PARTS (COUNT NOUNS)	THE WHOLE (A NONCOUNT NOUN)	
(c) chairs, tables, beds, etc.	furniture	Noncount nouns usually refer to a whole group of things that is made up of many individual parts, a whole category made up of different varieties. For example, some common noncount nouns are *furniture*, *mail*, *money*, *fruit*, and *jewelry*.

(d) letters, postcards, bills, etc.	mail	A language is not always logical. For instance:
		   *I had some **corn** for dinner.* (noncount)
		   *I had some **peas** for dinner.* (count)
		 Both **corn** and **peas** express a larger whole made up of smaller parts, but **corn** is a noncount noun and **pea** is a count noun.
		   ***Vegetables** are good for you.* (count)
		   ***Fruit** is good for you.* (noncount)
		 Both **vegetables** and **fruit** describe whole categories of food, but one is count and the other noncount.

(e) pennies, nickels, dollars, etc.	money	

(f) apples, bananas, oranges, etc.	fruit	Logically, you can count furniture. But in grammar, you cannot count furniture. For example: *I see a table and a bed.*
		   CORRECT: *I see some furniture.*
		   INCORRECT: *I see two furnitures.*

(g) rings, bracelets, necklaces, etc.	jewelry	

*A noncount noun is also sometimes called a *mass noun*.

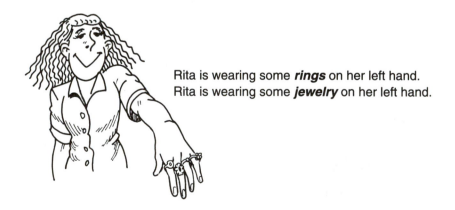

Rita is wearing some **rings** on her left hand.
Rita is wearing some **jewelry** on her left hand.

8-3 MORE NONCOUNT NOUNS

<table>
<tr><td colspan="2">(a) LIQUIDS</td><td colspan="4">SOLIDS and SEMI-SOLIDS</td><td>GASES</td></tr>
<tr><td>beer</td><td>milk</td><td>bread</td><td>meat</td><td>chalk</td><td>rubber</td><td>air</td></tr>
<tr><td>blood</td><td>oil</td><td>butter</td><td>beef</td><td>copper</td><td>silver</td><td>fog</td></tr>
<tr><td>coffee</td><td>shampoo</td><td>cheese</td><td>chicken</td><td>cotton</td><td>soap</td><td>oxygen</td></tr>
<tr><td>cream</td><td>soup</td><td>ice</td><td>fish</td><td>glass</td><td>tin</td><td>pollution</td></tr>
<tr><td>gasoline</td><td>tea</td><td>ice cream</td><td>ham</td><td>gold</td><td>toothpaste</td><td>smog</td></tr>
<tr><td>honey</td><td>water</td><td>lettuce</td><td>lamb</td><td>iron</td><td>wood</td><td>smoke</td></tr>
<tr><td>juice</td><td>wine</td><td>toast</td><td>pork</td><td>paper</td><td>wool</td><td>steam</td></tr>
</table>

(b) **NATURAL PHENOMENA** (things that occur in nature)

weather	lightning	darkness
rain	thunder	light
snow	humidity	sunshine

(c) **ABSTRACTIONS** (An abstraction is something that has no physical form. A person cannot touch it.)

anger	enjoyment	happiness	ignorance	luck	recreation
beauty	entertainment	hate	intelligence	patience	research
confidence	experience	health	justice	peace	stupidity
courage	fun	help	knowledge	poverty	time
cowardice	generosity	honesty	laughter	pride	violence
education	greed	hospitality	love	progress	wealth

Ann likes **milk**. She drinks a lot of **milk**.
(INCORRECT: *She drinks a lot of milks.*)

8-4 NOUNS THAT CAN BE COUNT OR NONCOUNT

Quite a few nouns can be used as either noncount or count nouns. Examples of both noncount and count usages for some common nouns follow:

NOUN	USED AS **NONCOUNT** NOUN	USED AS A **COUNT** NOUN
glass	(a) Windows are made of **glass**.	(b) I drank **a glass** of water.
		(c) Janet wears **glasses** when she reads.
hair	(d) Rita has brown **hair**.	(e) There's **a hair** on my jacket.
iron	(f) **Iron** is a metal.	(g) I pressed my shirt with **an iron**.
light	(h) I opened the curtain to let in **some light**.	(i) Please turn off **the lights** (lamps).
paper	(j) I need **some paper** to write a letter.	(k) I wrote **a paper** for Prof. Lee.
		(l) I bought **a paper** (a newspaper).
time	(m) How **much time** do you need to finish your work?	(n) How **many times** have you been in Mexico?
work	(o) I have **some work** to do tonight.	(p) That painting is **a work** of art.
coffee	(q) I had **some coffee** after dinner.	(r) **Two coffees**, please.
chicken fish lamb	(s) I had **some chicken/some fish/some lamb** for dinner.	(t) She drew a picture of **a chicken/a fish/a lamb**.

a little chicken a little chicken a few chickens

a big chicken a lot of chicken a lot of chickens

8-5 USING UNITS OF MEASURE WITH NONCOUNT NOUNS

(a) I had some tea.	To mention a specific quantity of a noncount noun, speakers use units of measure such as *two cups of* or *one piece of*. A unit of measure usually describes the container (e.g., *a cup of, a bowl of*) the amount (*a pound of, a quart of*),* or the shape (*a bar of soap, a sheet of paper*).
(b) I had **two cups of** tea.	
(c) I ate some toast.	
(d) I ate **one piece of** toast.	

*Weight measure: *one pound = 0.45 kilograms/kilos*   Liquid measure: *one quart = 0.95 litres/liters*
four quarts = one gallon = 3.8 litres/liters

I bought **a pound of** coffee,
a pair of shoes.
a tube of toothpaste,
two rolls of film,
a loaf of bread, and
a jar of mustard.

SHOPPING LIST
coffee
chicken or steak
potatoes
rice
shoes
toothpaste
bath soap
light bulbs
notebook paper
(rolls of) film
bread
mustard

8-6 GUIDELINES FOR ARTICLE USAGE

	USING *A* OR Ø (NO ARTICLE)		USING *A* OR *SOME*
SINGULAR COUNT NOUNS	(a) ***A dog*** makes a good pet. (b) ***A banana*** is yellow. (c) ***A pencil*** contains lead.	A speaker uses ***a*** with a singular count noun when s/he is making a generalization. In (a): The speaker is talking about any dog, all dogs, dogs in general.	(j) I saw ***a dog*** in my yard. (k) Mary ate ***a banana***. (l) I need ***a pencil***.
PLURAL COUNT NOUNS	(d) Ø ***Dogs*** make good pets. (e) Ø ***Bananas*** are yellow. (f) Ø ***Pencils*** contain lead.	A speaker uses no article (Ø) with a plural count noun when s/he is making a generalization.* In (d): The speaker is talking about any dog, all dogs, dogs in general. Note: (a) and (d) have the same meaning.	(m) I saw ***some dogs*** in my yard. (n) Mary bought ***some bananas***. (o) Bob has ***some pencils*** in his pocket.
NONCOUNT NOUNS	(g) Ø ***Fruit*** is good for you. (h) Ø ***Coffee*** contains caffeine. (i) I like Ø ***music***.	A speaker uses no article (Ø) with a noncount noun when s/he is making a generalization.* In (g): The speaker is talking about any fruit, all fruit, fruit in general.	(p) I bought ***some fruit***. (q) Bob drank ***some coffee***. (r) Would you like to listen to ***some music***?

*Sometimes a speaker uses an expression of quantity (e.g., ***almost all, most, some***) when s/he makes a generalization: *Almost all dogs make good pets. Most dogs are friendly. Some dogs have short hair.*

	USING _THE_	

A speaker uses **_a_** with a singular count noun when s/he is talking about one thing (or person) that is not specific.
 	
In (j): The speaker is saying, ''I saw one dog (not two dogs, some dogs, many dogs). It wasn't a specific dog (e.g., your dog, the neighbor's dog, that dog). It was only one dog out of the whole group of animals called dogs.''
	(s) Did you feed **_the dog_**?
	(t) I had a banana and an apple. I gave **_the banana_** to Mary.
	(u) **_The pencil_** on that desk is Jim's.
	(v) **_The sun_** is shining.
	(w) Please close **_the door_**.
	(x) Mary is in **_the kitchen_**.
		The is used in front of:
		  singular count nouns: _the dog_
		  plural count nouns: _the dogs_
		  noncount nouns: _the fruit_
		
		A speaker uses **_the_** (not **_a_**, Ø, or **_some_**) when the speaker and the listener are thinking about the same specific thing(s) or person(s).
		
		In (s): The speaker and the listener are thinking about the same specific dog. The listener knows which dog the speaker is talking about: the dog that they own, the dog that they feed every day. There is only one dog that the speaker could possibly be talking about.

A speaker often uses **_some_**** with a plural count noun when s/he is talking about things (or people) that are not specific. In (m): The speaker is saying, ''I saw more than one dog. They weren't specific dogs (e.g., your dogs, the neighbor's dogs, those dogs). The exact number of dogs isn't important (two dogs, five dogs); I'm simply saying that I saw an indefinite number of dogs.''	(y) Did you feed **_the dogs_**? (z) I had some bananas and some apples. I gave **_the bananas_** to Mary. (aa) **_The pencils_** on that desk are Jim's. (bb) Please turn off **_the lights_**.	In (t): A speaker uses **_the_** when s/he mentions a noun the second time. First mention: _I had **a** banana_ . . . Second mention: _I gave **the** banana_ . . . In the second mention, the listener now knows which banana the speaker is talking about: the banana the speaker had (not the banana John had, not the banana in that bowl).
A speaker often uses **_some_**** with a noncount noun when s/he is talking about something that is not specific. In (p): The speaker is saying, ''I bought an indefinite amount of fruit. The exact amount isn't important information (e.g., two pounds of fruit, four bananas and two apples). And I'm not talking about specific fruit (e.g., that fruit, the fruit in that bowl.)''	(cc) **_The fruit_** in this bowl is ripe. (dd) I drank some coffee and some milk. **_The coffee_** was hot. (ee) I can't hear you. **_The music_** is too loud. (ff) **_The air_** is cold today.	

In addition to **_some_, a speaker might use **_several, a few, a lot of,_** _etc._ with a plural count noun, or **_a little, a lot of,_** _etc._ with a noncount noun. (See Chart 8-1.)

DIALOGUE 1:

A: **A dog** makes a good pet.   B: I agree.

DIALOGUE 2:

A: I saw **a dog** in my yard.

DIALOGUE 4:

A: **Dogs** make good pets.   B: I agree.

DIALOGUE 5:

A: I saw **some dogs** in my yard.

DIALOGUE 7:

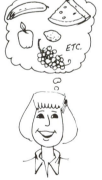

A: **Fruit** is good for you.   B: I agree.

DIALOGUE 8:

A: I ate **some fruit**.

DIALOGUE 3:

B: Oh?

A: Did you feed *the dog*?

B: Yes.

DIALOGUE 6:

B: Oh?

A: Did you feed *the dogs*?

B: Yes.

DIALOGUE 9:

B: Oh?

A: *The fruit* in this bowl is ripe.

B: Good.

8-7 USING EXPRESSIONS OF QUANTITY AS PRONOUNS

Expressions of quantity are words that describe the number or amount of a noun. 　　　　Examples of common expressions of quantity: *some, any, many, much, a lot (of), a few,* 　　　　　　　　　　　　　　　　　*a little, two, a couple (of), three, several, etc.* Expressions of quantity are usually used in front of a noun (e.g., *some paper, a lot of fruit*). They can also be used alone—without a noun—when the meaning is clear, i.e., when both speaker and listener know what the expression of quantity refers to. These expressions function as pronouns.	
(a) A: I need some yellow paper. 　　B: I don't have ***any***. Ask Matt. I think he 　　　 has ***some***.	In (a): ***any*** and ***some*** are used without a noun. It is clearly understood that: 　　*any　= any yellow paper* 　　*some = some yellow paper**
(b) A: I understand you're a baseball fan. 　　　Have you gone to a lot of baseball 　　　games? 　　B: Yes. I've gone to ***many***. I saw ***three*** just 　　　last week.	In (b): *many= many baseball games* 　　　 *three = three baseball games*

*In general, *any* is used in negative sentences; *some* is used in affirmative sentences.

8-8 NONSPECIFIC OBJECT PRONOUNS: *SOME, ANY,* AND *ONE*

(a) A: I need *some blank tapes*. (nonspecific) 　　B: I don't have ***any***, but Jack has ***some***. (b) A: Where are *the blank tapes* that were on 　　　my desk? (specific) 　　B: Rita has ***them***.	Object pronouns for PLURAL COUNT NOUNS: 　　nonspecific → ***some*** or ***any*** 　　specific → ***them*** In (a): The speakers are not talking about specific tapes. In (b): The speakers are talking about specific tapes, the tapes SPEAKER A left on her desk.
(c) A: I need *a blank tape*. (nonspecific) 　　B: I think you can get ***one*** from Jack. (d) A: Where's ***the blank tape*** that was on my 　　　desk? (specific) 　　B: Rita has ***it***.	Object pronouns for SINGULAR COUNT NOUNS: 　　nonspecific → ***one*** 　　specific → ***it, her, him***
(e) A: Would you like *some coffee*? (nonspecific) 　　B: No thanks, I just had ***some***. I don't want 　　　***any*** right now. (f) A: Your cup is empty. What happened to 　　　*your coffee*? (specific) 　　B: I drank ***it***.	Object pronouns for NONCOUNT COUNT NOUNS: 　　nonspecific → ***some*** or ***any*** 　　specific → ***it***

CHAPTER 9
Connecting Ideas

9-1 CONNECTING IDEAS WITH *AND*

When **and** connects only two items within a sentence, NO COMMAS are used. When **and** connects three or more items in a series in a sentence, commas are used.	

(a) I saw a *cat* **and** a *mouse.*
(b) I saw a *cat,* a *mouse,* **and** a *rat.*
    I saw a *cat,* a *mouse,* a *rat,* **and** a *dog.*
 	
(c) I *opened* the door **and** *walked* into the room.
(d) I *opened* the door, *walked* into the room, **and** *sat* down at my desk.
 	
(e) Their flag is *green* **and** *black.*
(f) Their flag is *green,* *black,* **and** *yellow.*
	In (a): **and** connects two nouns:
	    cat + *mouse* = NO COMMAS
	In (b): **and** connects three or more nouns, so commas are used.*
	In (c): NO COMMAS are used because **and** connects only two verbs (*opened* + *walked*).
	In (d): Commas are used because **and** connects three verbs (*opened* + *walked* + *sat*).
	In (e): **and** connects two adjectives (NO COMMAS).
	In (f): **and** connects three adjectives (commas).

When **and** connects two sentences, a comma is usually used.	

(g) I opened the door. She opened the window. (h) INCORRECT: I opened the door, she opened the window. (i) I opened the door, **and** she opened the window.	In (g): Two complete sentences (also called independent clauses) are separated by a period, NOT a comma.** (h) is incorrect because it has a comma between the two independent clauses. In (i): When **and** connects two independent clauses, a comma is usually used.

*In a series of three or more items, the comma before **and** is optional.
  ALSO CORRECT: *I saw a cat, a mouse and a rat.*

**Notice that a capital letter ("S" not "s") follows the period in (g). The first word in a new sentence is capitalized. See Chart 4-14 for more information about capitalization. Also note that a *period* is called a *full stop* in British English.

9-2 CONNECTING IDEAS WITH *BUT* AND *OR*

(a) I *went* to bed **but** *couldn't sleep.* (b) Is a lemon *sweet* **or** *sour?* (c) Did you order *coffee, tea,* **or** *milk?*	**And**, **but**, and **or** are called "conjunctions." **But** and **or** are used in the same ways as **and** (see 9-1). Notice: Only (c) uses commas.
(d) I dropped the vase, **but** it didn't break. (e) Do we have class on Monday, **or** is Monday a holiday?	Commas are usually used when **but** or **or** connects two complete sentences.* (*I dropped the vase* = a complete sentence.) (*it didn't break* = a complete sentence.)

*Sometimes with *but*, a period is used instead of a comma.
ALSO POSSIBLE: *I dropped the vase. But it didn't break.*

9-3 CONNECTING IDEAS WITH *SO*

(a) The room was dark, **so** I turned on a light.
 	
(b) I didn't study, **so** I failed the exam.
	So can be used as a conjunction. It is preceded by a comma. It connects the ideas in two independent clauses. **So** expresses **results**:
	    cause: *the room was dark*
	    result: *I turned on a light*

9-4 USING AUXILIARY VERBS AFTER *BUT* AND *AND*

(a) I *don't like coffee,* **but** my husband ***does***. (b) I *like tea,* **but** my husband ***doesn't***. (c) I *won't be here tomorrow,* **but** Sue ***will***. (d) I*'ve seen that movie,* **but** Joe ***hasn't***. (e) He *isn't here,* **but** she ***is***.*	After **but** and **and**, often a main verb is not repeated. Instead, only an auxiliary verb is used. The auxiliary is a substitute for the main verb phrase. The auxiliary after **but** and **and** has the same tense or modal as the main verb. In (a): *does* = *likes coffee.* The auxiliary *does* (simple present) is the substitute for the main verb phrase (simple present).
(f) I *don't like coffee,* **and** Ed ***doesn't*** either. (g) I *like tea,* **and** Kate ***does*** too. (h) I *won't be here,* **and** he ***won't*** either. (i) I*'ve seen that movie,* **and** Pat ***has*** too. (j) He *isn't here,* **and** Anna ***isn't*** either.	

	Notice in the examples:
	
	    negative + **but** + *affirmative*
	    affirmative + **but** + *negative*
	
	    negative + **and** + *negative*
	    affirmative + **and** + *affirmative*

*A verb is not contracted with a pronoun at the end of a sentence after **but** and **and**:
    CORRECT: . . . *but she is.*
    INCORRECT: . . . *but she's.*

AND . . . TOO
 	
AND SO . . .
	(a) Sue likes milk,
	   AND + S + *aux* + **TOO**
	   and **Tom** **does** **too.**
	(b) Sue likes milk,
	   AND + **SO** + *aux* + S
	   and **so** **does** **Tom.**
		(a) and (b) have the same meaning.
		
		Notice in (b): After ***and so*** . . ., the auxiliary verb (*aux*) comes before the subject (S).

AND . . . EITHER
 	
AND NEITHER . . .
	(c) Mary doesn't like milk,
	   AND + S + *aux* + **EITHER**
	   and **John** **doesn't** **either.**
	(d) Mary doesn't like milk,
	   AND + **NEITHER** + *aux* + S
	   and **neither** **does** **John.**
		(c) and (d) have the same meaning.
		
		Notice in (d): After ***and neither*** . . . , the auxiliary verb comes before the subject.
		
		Notice in (c): A negative auxiliary verb is used with ***and . . . either.*** In (d): An affirmative auxiliary verb is used with ***and neither*** . . . .

(e) A: I'm hungry.
   B: ***I am too***.
(g) A: I don't like hot dogs.
   B: ***I don't either***.
	(f) A: I'm hungry.
	   B: ***So am I***.
	(h) A: I don't like hot dogs.
	   B: ***Neither do I***.
		And is usually not used when there are two speakers.
		(e) and (f) have the same meaning.
		(g) and (h) have the same meaning.

(i) A: I'm hungry.
   B: ***Me too***. (*informal*)
	(j) A: I don't like hot dogs.
	   B: ***Me neither***. (*informal*)
		Me too and ***me neither*** are often used in informal spoken English.

Whales are mammals, ***and so are porpoises***.

BLUE WHALE

PORPOISE

Whales are mammals, ***and porpoises are too***.

9-6 CONNECTING IDEAS WITH *BECAUSE*

(a) He drank water *because* he was thirsty.	*Because* expresses a cause; it gives a reason. Why did he drink water? Reason: he was thirsty.
(b) MAIN CLAUSE: *He drank water.*	A main clause is a complete sentence: *He drank water.* = a complete sentence.
(c) ADVERB CLAUSE: *because he was thirsty*	An adverb clause is NOT a complete sentence: *because he was thirsty* = NOT a complete sentence. *Because* introduces an adverb clause: *because* + *subject* + *verb* = *an adverb clause.*

main clause   adverb clause
(d) ⌐He drank water⌐ ⌐*because he was thirsty.*⌐
          (no comma)
 	
     adverb clause   main clause
(e) ⌐*Because he was thirsty,*⌐ ⌐he drank water.⌐
         (comma)
	An adverb clause is connected to a main clause, as in (d) and (e).*
	In (d): **main clause + *no* comma + adverb clause.**
	In (e): **adverb clause + comma + main clause.**
	
	(d) and (e) have exactly the same meaning.

(f) INCORRECT: He drank water. Because he was thirsty.	(f) is incorrect: *because he was thirsty* cannot stand alone as a sentence that starts with a capital letter and ends with a period. It has to be connected to a main clause as in (d) and (e).

*See Chart 2-8 for a discussion of other adverb clauses. "Time clauses" are adverb clauses that are introduced by *when, after, before,* and *while.*

Debbie woke up in the morning with a sore throat *because she had cheered loudly at the basketball game.*

9-7 CONNECTING IDEAS WITH *EVEN THOUGH/ALTHOUGH*

(a) ***Even though*** *I was hungry,* I did not eat. I did not eat ***even though*** *I was hungry.* (b) ***Although*** *I was hungry,* I did not eat. I did not eat ***although*** *I was hungry.*	*Even though* and *although* introduce an adverb clause. (a) and (b) have the same meaning. They mean: *I was hungry, but I did not eat.*
COMPARE: (c)　　*Because I was hungry, I ate.* (d) *Even though I was hungry, I did not eat.*	*Because* expresses an expected result. *Even though/although* expresses an unexpected or opposite result.

TIM　　　　MATT　　　　DAN　　　　NICK

Even though / although Tim is fairly tall, he can't reach the ceiling.

Because Matt is very tall, he can reach the ceiling.

Because Dan isn't as tall as Matt, he can't reach the ceiling.

Even though / Although Nick isn't tall, he can reach the ceiling by standing on a chair.

9-8 PHRASAL VERBS (SEPARABLE)

(a) We **put off** our trip.	In (a): **put off** = *a phrasal verb.** *A phrasal verb* = a verb and a particle that together have a special meaning. For example, **put off** means "postpone." *A particle* = a preposition (e.g., *off, on*) or an adverb (e.g., *away, back*) that is used in a phrasal verb.
(b) We *put **off** our trip.* (c) We *put our trip **off**.* (d) I *turned **on** the light.* (e) I *turned the light **on**.*	Many phrasal verbs are **separable.**** In other words, a NOUN can either follow or come between (separate) the verb and the particle. (b) and (c) have the same meaning. (d) and (e) have the same meaning.

(f) We *put **it** off.*
(g) I *turned **it** on.*
	If a phrasal verb is **separable**, the PRONOUN always comes between the verb and the particle; the pronoun never follows the particle.
	    INCORRECT: *We put off it.*
	    INCORRECT: *I turned on it.*

SOME COMMON PHRASAL VERBS (SEPARABLE)

figure out . . . . *find the solution to a problem*
hand in . . . . *give homework, test papers, etc., to a teacher*
hand out . . . . *give something to this person, then that person, then another person, etc.*
look up . . . . *look for information in a dictionary, a telephone directory, an encyclopedia, etc.*
make up . . . . *invent a story*
pick up . . . . *lift*
put down . . . . *stop holding or carrying*
put off . . . . *postpone*
put on . . . . *put clothes on one's body*
take off . . . . *remove clothes from one's body*
throw away⎫
throw out ⎭ . . . . . *put in the trash, discard*
turn off . . . . *stop a machine or a light*
turn on . . . . *start a machine or a light*
wake up . . . . *stop sleeping*
write down . . . . . . *write a note on a piece of paper*

*Phrasal verbs are also called *two-word verbs* and *three-word verbs*.

Some phrasal verbs are **nonseparable. Chart 9-9 will discuss nonseparable phrasal verbs. See Appendix 2 for a list of phrasal verbs.

I ***threw away*** yesterday's newspaper.

9-9 PHRASAL VERBS (NONSEPARABLE)

(a) I **ran into Bob** at the bank yesterday.	If a phrasal verb is **nonseparable**, a noun or pronoun follows (never precedes) the particle.
(b) I saw Bob yesterday. I **ran into him** at the bank.	INCORRECT: *I ran Bob into at the bank.*
	INCORRECT: *I ran him into at the bank.*

SOME COMMON PHRASAL VERBS (NONSEPARABLE)

call on......... *ask to speak in class*
get over .... *recover from an illness*
run into .... *meet by chance*
get on .... *enter* ⎫
get off .... *leave* ⎬| *a bus, an airplane, a train, a subway, a bicycle*
get in .... *enter* ⎫
get out of ...... *leave* ⎬ *a car, a taxi*

CHAPTER 10
Gerunds and Infinitives

10-1 GERUNDS AND INFINITIVES: INTRODUCTION

noun (a) I enjoy music.	**S V O** *I enjoy **something**. (something* = the object of the verb.) The object of a verb is usually a noun or pronoun, as in (a). The object of a verb can also be a gerund. A gerund is *the **-ing** form of a verb.*★ It is used as a noun.
gerund (b) I enjoy ***listening*** to music.	
gerund phrase (c) I enjoy ***listening to music***.	In (b): ***listening*** is a gerund. It is the object of the verb ***enjoy***.
noun (d) I want a sandwich.	**S V O** *I want **something**. (something* = the object of the verb.) In (d): The object of the verb is a noun (*a sandwich*).
infinitive (e) I want ***to eat*** a sandwich.	The object of a verb can also be an infinitive. An infinitive is ***to*** + *the simple form of a verb.* In (e): ***to eat*** is an infinitive. It is the object of the verb ***want***.
infinitive phrase (f) I want ***to eat*** a sandwich.	
(g) I *enjoy **going*** to the beach.	Some verbs (e.g., *enjoy*) are followed by gerunds. (See 10-2.)
(h) Ted *wants **to go*** to the beach.	Some verbs (e.g., *want*) are followed by infinitives. (See 10-4.)
(i) It *began **raining***. It *began **to rain***.	Some verbs (e.g., *begin*) are followed by either gerunds or infinitives. (See 10-5.)

★The **-ing** form of a verb can be used as a present participle:
  *I **am listening** to the teacher right now.* (***listening*** = a present participle, used in the present progressive)
  The -ing form of a verb can be used as a gerund:
  *I enjoy **listening** to music.* (***listening*** = a gerund, used as the object of the verb ***enjoy***)

10-2 VERB + GERUND

COMMON VERBS FOLLOWED BY GERUNDS		Gerunds are used as the objects of the verbs in the list. The list also contains phrasal verbs (e.g., *put off*) that are followed by gerunds.
enjoy	(a) I *enjoy working* in my garden.	
finish	(b) Bob *finished studying* at midnight.	
*stop**	(c) It *stopped raining* a few minutes ago.	These verbs are NOT followed by infinitives.* For example:
quit	(d) David *quit smoking*.	INCORRECT: *I enjoy to work.*
mind	(e) Would you *mind opening* the window?	INCORRECT: *Bob finished to study.*
postpone	(f) I *postponed doing* my homework.	INCORRECT: *I'm thinking to go to Hawaii.*
put off	(g) I *put off doing* my homework.	
keep	(h) *Keep working*. Don't stop.	
keep on	(i) *Keep on working*. Don't stop.	
consider	(j) I'*m considering going* to Hawaii.	
think about	(k) I'*m thinking about going* to Hawaii.	
discuss	(l) They *discussed getting* a new car.	See Chart 2-5 for the spelling of *-ing* verb forms.
talk about	(m) They *talked about getting* a new car.	
(n) I considered *not going* to class.		Negative form: *not* + *gerund*.

*The object following *stop* is a gerund, NOT an infinitive. INCORRECT: *It stopped to rain.*
  But in a special circumstance, *stop* can be followed by an infinitive of purpose: *in order to* (see Chart 10-11). *While I was walking down the hall, I dropped my pen.* **I *stopped to pick*** it up. = *I* ***stopped walking in order to pick*** *it up.*

10-3 GO + -ING

(a) **Did** you **go shopping** yesterday?
 (b) I **went swimming** last week.
 (c) Bob **hasn't gone fishing** in years.
	Go is followed by a gerund in certain idiomatic expressions about activities.
	 Notice: There is no **to** between **go** and the gerund.
	     INCORRECT: *Did you go to shopping?*
	     CORRECT: *Did you go shopping?*

COMMON EXPRESSIONS WITH *GO* + *-ING*

go boating	*go hiking*	*go sightseeing*
go bowling	*go jogging*	*go skating*
go camping	*go running*	*go (water) skiing*
go dancing	*go sailing*	*go skydiving*
go fishing	*go (window) shopping*	*go swimming*

10-4 VERB + INFINITIVE

(a) Tom **offered to lend** me some money. (b) I've **decided to buy** a new car.	Some verbs are followed by an infinitive: AN INFINITIVE = **to** + *the simple form of a verb.*
(c) I've **decided not to keep** my old car.	Negative form: **not** + *infinitive.*

COMMON VERBS FOLLOWED BY INFINITIVES

want	*hope*	*decide*	*seem*	*learn* (*how*)
need	*expect*	*promise*	*appear*	*try*
would like	*plan*	*offer*	*pretend*	
would love	*intend*	*agree*		(*can't*) *afford*
	mean	*refuse*	*forget*	(*can't*) *wait*

I'd really like **to climb** to the top of an active volcano and **(to) look** inside the crater.

10-5 VERB + GERUND OR INFINITIVE

(a) It *began* **to rain**. (b) It *began* **raining**.	Some verbs are followed by either an infinitive or a gerund. Usually there is no difference in meaning. (a) and (b) have the same meaning.

COMMON VERBS FOLLOWED BY EITHER A GERUND OR AN INFINITIVE

begin	*like*★	*hate*
start	*love*★	*can't stand*
continue		

★COMPARE: **Like** and **love** can be followed by either a gerund or an infinitive:
I like going/to go to movies. I love playing/to play chess.

Would like and **would love** are followed by infinitives:
I would like to go to a movie tonight. I'd love to play a game of chess right now.

10-6 UNCOMPLETED INFINITIVES

(a) I've never met Rita, but *I'd like **to***. (b) INCORRECT: I've never met Rita, but I'd like. (c) INCORRECT: I've never met Rita, but I'd like it. (d) INCORRECT: I've never met Rita, but I'd like to do.	In (a): *I'd like **to*** = an uncompleted infinitive; *I'd like **to meet Rita*** = the understood completion. An infinitive phrase is not completed following ***to*** when the meaning is clearly understood to repeat the idea that came immediately before. Uncompleted infinitives follow the verbs in Charts 10-4 and 10-5.
(e) I don't want to leave, but *I have **to***. (f) Sam doesn't go to school here, but *he used **to***.	Uncompleted infinitives are also common with these auxiliaries: *have to, be going to, used to,* and *ought to.*

10-7 PREPOSITION + GERUND

(a) Kate *insisted **on coming*** with us. (b) We're *excited **about going*** to Tahiti. (c) I *apologized **for being*** late.	A preposition is followed by a gerund, not an infinitive. In (a): preposition (*on*) + gerund (*coming*)

Instead ***of cutting*** his own hair, Jake should go to a barber.

10-8 USING *BY* AND *WITH* TO EXPRESS HOW SOMETHING IS DONE

(a) Pat turned off the tape recorder *by pushing* the stop button.	*By* + *a gerund* is used to express how something is done.
(b) Mary goes to work *by bus*. (c) Andrea stirred her coffee *with a spoon*.	*By* or *with* followed by a noun is also used to express how something is done.

BY IS USED FOR MEANS OF TRANSPORTATION AND COMMUNICATION:

by	*by subway*★★	*by mail*	*by air*
(air)plane★	*by taxi*	*by (tele)phone*	*by land*
by boat	*by train*	*by fax*	*by sea*
by bus	*by foot* (OR *on foot*)		
by car			

OTHERS:

by chance
by choice
by mistake
by check (but *in cash*)
by hand★★★

WITH IS USED FOR INSTRUMENTS OR PARTS OF THE BODY:

I cut down the tree *with an ax* (by using an ax).
I swept the floor *with a broom*.
She pointed to a spot on the map *with her finger*.

★*airplane* = American English *aeroplane* = British English
★★*by subway* = American English *by underground, by tube* = British English

★★★The expression *by hand* is usually used to mean that something was made by a person, not by a machine: *This rug was made by hand*. (A person, not a machine, made this rug.) COMPARE: *I touched his shoulder with my hand*.

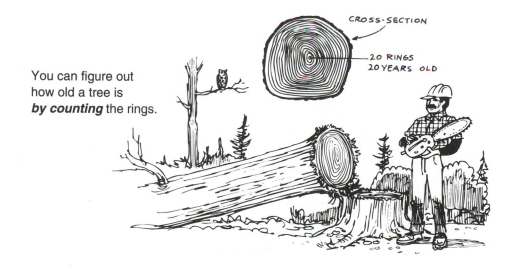

CROSS-SECTION

20 RINGS
20 YEARS OLD

You can figure out
how old a tree is
by counting the rings.

10-9 USING GERUNDS AS SUBJECTS; USING *IT* + INFINITIVE

(a) ***Riding*** horses is fun. (b) ***It*** is fun ***to ride*** horses.	(a) and (b) have the same meaning. In (a): A gerund (*riding*) is the subject of the sentence.* Notice: The verb (*is*) is singular because a gerund is singular.
(c) ***Coming*** to class on time is important. (d) ***It*** is important ***to come*** to class on time.	In (b): The word ***it*** is used as the subject of the sentence. The word ***it*** has the same meaning as the infinitive phrase at the end of the sentence: ***it*** means *to ride horses*.

*It is also correct (but less common) to use an infinitive as the subject of a sentence: *To ride horses is fun.*

10-10 *IT* + INFINITIVE: USING *FOR (SOMEONE)*

(a) *You* should study hard. (b) It is important ***for you*** to study hard. (c) *Mary* should study hard. (d) It is important ***for Mary*** to study hard. (e) *We* don't have to go to the meeting. (f) It isn't necessary ***for us*** to go to the meeting. (g) *A dog* can't talk. (h) It is impossible ***for a dog*** to talk.	(a) and (b) have a similar meaning. Notice the pattern in (b): ***it is*** + *adjective* + ***for*** *(someone)* + *infinitive phrase*

It's traditional ***for my family***
to eat turkey on Thanksgiving Day.

10-11 INFINITIVE OF PURPOSE: USING *IN ORDER TO*

Why did you go to the post office? (a) I went to the post office *because I wanted to mail a letter.* (b) I went to the post office **in order to mail** *a letter.* (c) I went to the post office **to mail** *a letter.*	***In order to*** expresses purpose. ***In order to*** answers the question "Why?"
	In (c): ***in order*** is frequently omitted. (a), (b) and (c) have the same meaning.
(d) I went to the post office ***for*** *some stamps.* (e) I went to the post office ***to buy*** *some stamps.* (f) INCORRECT: I went to the post office for to buy some stamps. (g) INCORRECT: I went to the post office for buying some stamps.	***For*** is also used to express purpose, but it is a preposition and is followed by a noun phrase, as in (d).

I stood in the doorway of a store *(in order) to get* out of the rain while I was waiting for the bus.

10-12 USING INFINITIVES WITH *TOO* AND *ENOUGH*

TOO + ADJECTIVE + (FOR SOMEONE) + INFINITIVE (a) A piano is **too** *heavy* **to** *lift*. (b) That box is **too** *heavy* **for** *me* **to** *lift*. (c) That box is **too** *heavy* **for** *Bob* **to** *lift*.	Infinitives often follow expressions with *too*. *Too* comes in front of an adjective. In the speaker's mind, the use of *too* implies a negative result. COMPARE: *The box is too heavy. I can't lift it.* *The box is very heavy, but I can lift it.*
ENOUGH + NOUN + INFINITIVE (d) I don't have **enough** *money* **to** *buy* that car. (e) Did you have **enough** *time* **to** *finish* the test?	Infinitives often follow expressions with *enough*. *Enough* comes in front of a noun.* *Enough* follows an adjective.
ADJECTIVE + ENOUGH + INFINITIVE (f) Jimmy isn't *old* **enough** **to** *go* to school. (g) Are you *hungry* **enough** **to** *eat* three sandwiches?	

*****Enough** can also follow a noun: *I don't have **money** enough to buy that car.* In everyday English, however, *enough* usually comes in front of a noun.

10-13 MORE PHRASAL VERBS (SEPARABLE)*

ask out	*ask someone to go on a date*
call back	*return a telephone call*
call off	*cancel*
call up	*make a telephone call*
give back	*return something to someone*
hang up	*(1) hang on a hanger or a hook; (2) end a telephone call*
pay back	*return money to someone*
put away	*put something in its usual or proper place*
put back	*return something to its original place*
put out	*extinguish (stop) a fire, a cigarette, a cigar*
shut off	*stop a machine or light, turn off*
try on	*put on clothing to see if it fits*
turn down	*decrease the volume*
turn up	*increase the volume*

*See 9-8 and 9-9 for more information about phrasal verbs.

This is a nice-looking coat.
Why don't you try *it on*?

CHAPTER *11*

Passive Sentences

11-1 ACTIVE SENTENCES AND PASSIVE SENTENCES

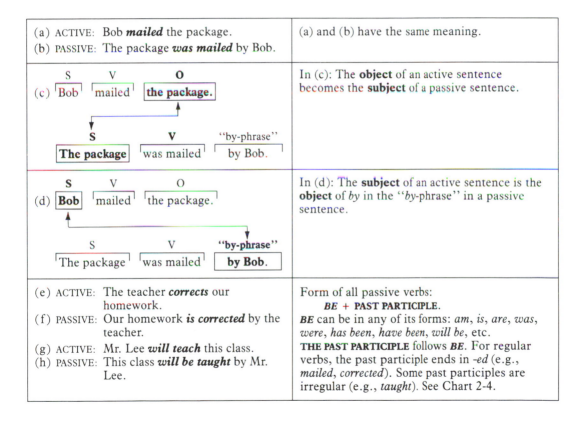

(a) ACTIVE: Bob *mailed* the package. (b) PASSIVE: The package *was mailed* by Bob.	(a) and (b) have the same meaning.
(c)	In (c): The **object** of an active sentence becomes the **subject** of a passive sentence.
(d)	In (d): The **subject** of an active sentence is the **object** of *by* in the "*by*-phrase" in a passive sentence.
(e) ACTIVE: The teacher *corrects* our homework. (f) PASSIVE: Our homework *is corrected* by the teacher. (g) ACTIVE: Mr. Lee *will teach* this class. (h) PASSIVE: This class *will be taught* by Mr. Lee.	Form of all passive verbs: *BE* + PAST PARTICIPLE. *BE* can be in any of its forms: *am, is, are, was, were, has been, have been, will be,* etc. THE PAST PARTICIPLE follows *BE*. For regular verbs, the past participle ends in *-ed* (e.g., *mailed, corrected*). Some past participles are irregular (e.g., *taught*). See Chart 2-4.

11-2   TENSE FORMS OF PASSIVE VERBS

Notice that all the passive verbs are formed with **BE** + **PAST PARTICIPLE**.				
TENSE	ACTIVE		PASSIVE	
SIMPLE PRESENT	The news	*surprises* me.	I	*am surprised* by the news.
	The news	*surprises* Sam.	Sam	*is surprised* by the news.
	The news	*surprises* us.	We	*are surprised* by the news.
SIMPLE PAST	The news	*surprised* me.	I	*was surprised* by the news.
	The news	*surprised* us.	We	*were surprised* by the news.
PRESENT PERFECT	Bob	*has mailed* the letter.	The letter	*has been mailed* by Bob.
	Bob	*has mailed* the letters.	The letters	*have been mailed* by Bob.
FUTURE	Bob	*will mail* the letter.	The letter	*will be mailed* by Bob.
	Bob *is going to mail* the letter.		The letter *is going to be mailed* by Bob.	

11-3   TRANSITIVE AND INTRANSITIVE VERBS

(a) **TRANSITIVE VERBS** 　　ACTIVE: Bob *mailed* the letter. 　　PASSIVE: The letter *was mailed* by Bob. (b) **INTRANSITIVE VERBS** 　　ACTIVE: An accident *happened*. 　　PASSIVE: (*not possible*) (c) INCORRECT: An accident was happened.	Only transitive verbs can be used in the passive. A transitive verb is a verb that is followed by an object. Examples: 　　　　**S**　　**V**　　　**O** 　　*Bob mailed the letter.* 　*Mr. Lee signed the check.* 　　*A cat killed the bird.*
	An intransitive verb is a verb that is not followed by an object. Example: 　　　　**S**　　　**V** 　*An accident happened.* 　　*John came to our house.* 　　　*I slept well last night.* An intransitive verb CANNOT be used in the passive.

11-4 USING THE "*BY*-PHRASE"

(a) This sweater *was made* **by my aunt**.	The "*by*-phrase" is used in passive sentences when it is important to know who performs an action. In (a): *by my aunt* is important information.
(b) That sweater *was made* in Korea. (*by someone*) (c) Spanish *is spoken* in Colombia. (*by people*) (d) That house *was built* in 1940. (*by someone*) (e) Rice *is grown* in many countries. (*by people*)	Uusually there is no "*by*-phrase" in a passive sentence. The passive is used when it is not known or not important to know exactly who performs an action. In (b): The exact person (or people) who made the sweater is not known and is not important to know, so there is no "*by*-phrase" in the passive sentence.

ACTIVE: Someone *filmed* many of the Tarzan movies in the rain forest in Puerto Rico.

"CAMERA! ACTION!"

PASSIVE: Many of the Tarzan movies *were filmed* in the rain forest in Puerto Rico. *(by someone)*

11-5 THE PASSIVE FORMS OF THE PRESENT AND PAST PROGRESSIVE

ACTIVE	PASSIVE	
The secretary *is copying* some letters.	(a) Some letters ***are being copied*** by the secretary.	Passive form of the present progressive:
Someone *is building* a new hospital.	(b) A new hospital ***is being built***.	$\left.\begin{array}{l}\textit{\textbf{am}}\\\textit{\textbf{is}}\\\textit{\textbf{are}}\end{array}\right\}$ + ***being*** + PAST PARTICIPLE
The secretary *was copying* some letters.	(c) Some letters ***were being copied*** by the secretary.	Passive form of the past progressive:
Someone *was building* a new hospital.	(d) A new hospital ***was being built***.	$\left.\begin{array}{l}\textit{\textbf{was}}\\\textit{\textbf{were}}\end{array}\right\}$ + ***being*** + PAST PARTICIPLE

ACTIVE: The dog ***is chasing*** the bear up a tree.

PASSIVE: The bear ***is being chased*** up a tree by the dog.

11-6 PASSIVE MODAL AUXILIARIES

ACTIVE MODAL AUXILIARIES	PASSIVE MODAL AUXILIARIES (MODAL + BE + PAST PARTICIPLE)	Modal auxiliaries are often used in the passive.
Bob *will mail* it. Bob *can mail* it. Bob *should mail* it. Bob *ought to mail* it. Bob *must mail* it. Bob *has to mail* it. Bob *may mail* it. Bob *might mail* it.	It *will be mailed* by Bob. It *can be mailed* by Bob. It *should be mailed* by Bob. It *ought to be mailed* by Bob. It *must be mailed* by Bob. It *has to be mailed* by Bob. It *may be mailed* by Bob. It *might be mailed* by Bob.	FORM: modal + *BE* + past participle See Chapter 5 for information about the meanings and uses of modal auxiliaries.

11-7 SUMMARY: PASSIVE VERB FORMS

REMINDER: All passive verbs are formed with *BE* + PAST PARTICIPLE.

ACTIVE			PASSIVE		
Dr. Gray	*helps*	Tom.	Tom	*is helped*	by Dr. Gray.
Dr. Gray	*is helping*	Tom.	Tom	*is being helped*	by Dr. Gray.
Dr. Gray	*has helped*	Tom.	Tom	*has been helped*	by Dr. Gray.
Dr. Gray	*helped*	Tom.	Tom	*was helped*	by Dr. Gray.
Dr. Gray	*was helping*	Tom.	Tom	*was being helped*	by Dr. Gray.
Dr. Gray	*had helped*	Tom.	Tom	*had been helped*	by Dr. Gray.
Dr. Gray	*is going to help*	Tom.	Tom	*is going to be helped*	by Dr. Gray.
Dr. Gray	*will help*	Tom.	Tom	*will be helped*	by Dr. Gray.
Dr. Gray	*can help*	Tom.	Tom	*can be helped*	by Dr. Gray.
Dr. Gray	*should help*	Tom.	Tom	*should be helped*	by Dr. Gray.
Dr. Gray	*ought to help*	Tom.	Tom	*ought to be helped*	by Dr. Gray.
Dr. Gray	*must help*	Tom.	Tom	*must be helped*	by Dr. Gray.
Dr. Gray	*has to help*	Tom.	Tom	*has to be helped*	by Dr. Gray.
Dr. Gray	*may help*	Tom.	Tom	*may be helped*	by Dr. Gray.
Dr. Gray	*might help*	Tom.	Tom	*might be helped*	by Dr. Gray.

11-8 USING PAST PARTICIPLES AS ADJECTIVES (STATIVE PASSIVE)

BE + ADJECTIVE (a) Paul *is* **young**. (b) Paul *is* **tall**. (c) Paul *is* **hungry**. **BE + PAST PARTICIPLE** (d) Paul *is* **married**. (e) Paul *is* **tired**. (f) Paul *is* **frightened**.	***Be*** can be followed by an adjective. The adjective describes or gives information about the subject of the sentence. ***Be*** can be followed by a past participle (the passive form). The past participle is often like an adjective. The past participle describes or gives information about the subject of the sentence. Past participles are used as adjectives in many common, everyday expressions.
(g) Paul *is married* **to** Susan. (h) Paul *was excited* **about** the game. (i) Paul *will be prepared* **for** the exam.	Often the past participles in these expressions are followed by particular prepositions + an object. For example: • ***married*** is followed by ***to*** (+ an object). • ***excited*** is followed by ***about*** (+ an object). • ***prepared*** is followed by ***for*** (+ an object).

SOME COMMON EXPRESSIONS WITH *BE* + PAST PARTICIPLE

1. *be acquainted (with)*	13. *be excited (about)*	25. *be opposed (to)*
2. *be bored (with, by)*	14. *be exhausted (from)*	26. *be pleased (with)*
3. *be broken*	15. *be finished (with)*	27. *be prepared (for)*
4. *be closed*	16. *be frightened (of, by)*	28. *be qualified (for)*
5. *be composed of*	17. *be gone (from)*	29. *be related (to)*
6. *be crowded (with)*	18. *be hurt*	30. *be satisfied (with)*
7. *be devoted (to)*	19. *be interested (in)*	31. *be scared (of, by)*
8. *be disappointed (in, with)*	20. *be involved (in)*	32. *be shut*
9. *be divorced (from)*	21. *be located in, south of, etc.*	33. *be spoiled*
10. *be done (with)*	22. *be lost*	34. *be terrified (of, by)*
11. *be drunk (on)*	23. *be made of*	35. *be tired (of, from)*
12. *be engaged (to)*	24. *be married (to)*	36. *be worried (about)*

*I'm **tired** *of* the cold weather. = *I've had enough cold weather. I want the weather to get warm.*
I'm **tired** *from* working hard all day. = *I'm exhausted because I worked hard all day.*

11-9 PARTICIPIAL ADJECTIVES: *-ED* vs. *-ING*

Indian art interests me.
(a) I am ***interested*** in Indian art.
    INCORRECT: I am interesting in Indian art.
(b) Indian art is ***interesting.***
    INCORRECT: Indian art is interested.
 	
    The news surprised Kate.
(c) Kate was ***surprised.***
(d) The news was ***surprising.***
	The past participle (*-ed*)* and the present participle (*-ing*) can be used as adjectives.
	In (a): The past participle (*interested*) describes how a person feels.
	In (b): The present participle (*interesting*) describes the ***cause*** of the feeling. The cause of the interest is Indian art.
	In (c): ''surprised'' describes how Kate felt.
	The past participle carries a passive meaning: *Kate was surprised **by the news**.*
	In (d): ''the news'' was the cause of the surprise.

*The past participle of regular verbs ends in *-ed*. Some verbs have irregular forms. See Chart 2-4.

The children went to a circus.
For them, the circus was ***exciting***.
The ***excited*** children jumped up and down.

11-10 *GET* + ADJECTIVE; *GET* + PAST PARTICIPLE

GET + ADJECTIVE (a) I **am getting hungry**. Let's eat. (b) Eric **got nervous** before the job interview.	**Get** can be followed by an adjective. **Get** gives the idea of change—the idea of becoming, beginning to be, growing to be. In (a): *I'm getting hungry = I wasn't hungry before, but now I'm beginning to be hungry.*
GET + PAST PARTICIPLE (c) I**'m getting tired**. Let's stop working. (d) Steve and Rita **got married** last month.	Sometimes **get** is followed by a past participle. The past participle after **get** is like an adjective; it describes the subject of the sentence.

GET + ADJECTIVE			GET + PAST PARTICIPLE		
get angry	get dry	get quiet	get acquainted	get drunk	get involved
get bald	get fat	get rich	get arrested	get engaged	get killed
get big	get full	get serious	get bored	get excited	get lost
get busy	get hot	get sick	get confused	get finished	get married
get close	get hungry	get sleepy	get crowded	get frightened	get scared
get cold	get interested	get thirsty	get divorced	get hurt	get sunburned
get dark	get late	get well	get done	get interested	get tired
get dirty	get nervous	get wet	get dressed	get invited	get worried
get dizzy	get old				

11-11 USING *BE USED/ACCUSTOMED TO* AND *GET USED/ACCUSTOMED TO*

(a) I **am used to** hot weather. (b) I **am accustomed to** hot weather. (c) I **am used to living** in a hot climate. (d) I **am accustomed to living** in a hot climate.	(a) and (b) have the same meaning: "Living in a hot climate is usual and normal for me. I'm familiar with what it is like to live in a hot climate. Hot weather isn't strange or different to me." Notice in (c) and (d): **to** (a preposition) is followed by the **-ing** form of a verb (a gerund).*
(e) I just moved from Florida to Alaska. I have never lived in a cold climate before, but I **am getting used to (accustomed to)** the cold weather here.	In (e): *I'm getting used to/accustomed to =* something is beginning to seem usual and normal to me.

*COMPARE: To express the habitual past (see 2-9), the infinitive form follows **used**: *I used to live in Chicago, but now I live in New York*. However, **be used to** is followed by a gerund: *I am used to living in a big city*.

NOTE: In both **used to** (habitual past) and **be used to**, the "d" is not pronounced in "used."

11-12   USING *BE SUPPOSED TO*

(a) Mike *is supposed to call* me tomorrow. (IDEA: I expect Mike to call me tomorrow.) (b) We *are supposed to write* a composition. (IDEA: The teacher expects us to write a composition). (c) It *is supposed to rain* today. (IDEA: People expect it to rain today.) (d) Alice *was supposed to be* home at ten. (IDEA: Someone expected Alice to be home at ten.)	*Be supposed to* is used to talk about an activity or event that is expected to occur. In (a): The idea of *is supposed to* is that Mike is expected (by me) to call. I asked him to call me. He promised to call me. I expect him to call me.
	NOTE: The present form of *be* is used for both future expectations and present expectations.

CHAPTER *12*
Adjective Clauses

12-1   ADJECTIVE CLAUSES: INTRODUCTION

ADJECTIVES	ADJECTIVE CLAUSES*
An **adjective** modifies a noun. "*Modify*" means to change a little. An adjective gives a little different meaning to a noun. It describes or gives information about a noun. (See Chart 4-4).	An **adjective clause** modifies a noun. It describes or gives information about a noun.
An adjective usually comes in front of a noun.	An adjective clause follows a noun.
(a) I met a *adjective* + *noun* **kind** man. (b) I met a *adjective* + *noun* **famous** man.	(c) I met a *noun* + *adjective clause* man **who is kind to everybody**. (d) I met a *noun* + *adjective clause* man **who is a famous poet**. (e) I met a *noun* + *adjective clause* man **who lives in Chicago**.

*Grammar terminology:

A **clause** is a structure that has a subject and a verb.

There are two kinds of clauses: independent and dependent. An **independent clause** is a main clause. It can stand alone as a sentence. A **dependent clause** must be connected to an independent clause. A dependent clause cannot stand alone as a sentence. An adjective clause is a dependent clause.

    I met a man = *an independent clause*

    who is kind to everybody = *a dependent clause*

The woman *who read my palm* predicted my future.

12-2 USING *WHO* AND *WHOM* IN ADJECTIVE CLAUSES

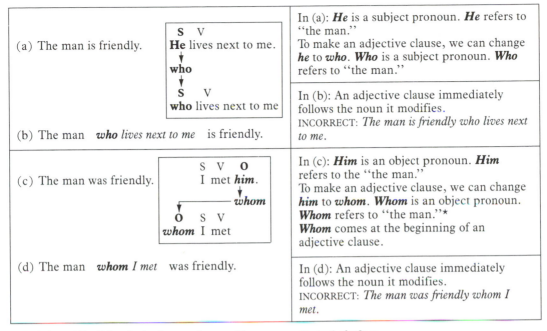

(a) The man is friendly.	**S V** **He** lives next to me. ↓ **who** ↓ **S V** **who** lives next to me	In (a): **He** is a subject pronoun. **He** refers to "the man." To make an adjective clause, we can change **he** to **who**. **Who** is a subject pronoun. **Who** refers to "the man."
(b) The man **who** *lives next to me* is friendly.		In (b): An adjective clause immediately follows the noun it modifies. INCORRECT: *The man is friendly who lives next to me.*
(c) The man was friendly.	**S V O** I met **him**. ↓ **whom** **O S V** **whom** I met	In (c): **Him** is an object pronoun. **Him** refers to the "the man." To make an adjective clause, we can change **him** to **whom**. **Whom** is an object pronoun. **Whom** refers to "the man."* **Whom** comes at the beginning of an adjective clause.
(d) The man **whom** *I met* was friendly.		In (d): An adjective clause immediately follows the noun it modifies. INCORRECT: *The man was friendly whom I met.*

*In informal English, **who** is often used as an object pronoun instead of **whom**:
FORMAL: *The man **whom** I met was friendly.*
INFORMAL: *The man **who** I met was friendly.*

12-3 USING *WHO*, *WHOM*, AND *THAT* IN ADJECTIVE CLAUSES

(a) The man is friendly.	**S V** **He** lives next to me. ↓ **who** **that**	In addition to **who**, we can use **that** as the subject of an adjective clause. (b) and (c) have the same meaning.
(b) The man **who** *lives next to me* is friendly. (c) The man **that** *lives next to me* is friendly.	**S V**	A subject pronoun cannot be omitted: INCORRECT: *The man lives next to me is friendly.* CORRECT: *The man who/that lives next to me is friendly.*
(d) The man was friendly.	**S V O** I met **him**. ↓ **whom** **that**	In addition to **whom**, we can use **that** as the object in an adjective clause. (e) and (f) have the same meaning.
(e) The man **whom** *I met* was friendly. (f) The man **that** *I met* was friendly. (g) The man **Ø** *I met* was friendly.	**O S V**	An object pronoun can be omitted from an adjective clause. (e), (f), and (g) have the same meaning. In (g): The symbol "Ø" means "nothing goes here."

12-4 USING *WHICH* AND *THAT* IN ADJECTIVE CLAUSES

<table>
<tr>
<td>

(a) The river is polluted. | **S** **V** / **It** flows through town. / ↓ / **which** **that**

        S **V**
(b) The river **which** *flows through town* is polluted.
(c) The river **that** *flows through town* is polluted.

</td>
<td>

Who and **whom** refer to people. **Which** refers to things. **That** can refer to either people or things.

</td>
</tr>
<tr>
<td></td>
<td>

In (a): To make an adjective clause, we can change *it* to **which** or **that**. *It*, **which**, and **that** all refer to a thing (the river).
(b) and (c) have the same meaning.

</td>
</tr>
<tr>
<td></td>
<td>

When **which** and **that** are used as the subject of an adjective clause, they CANNOT be omitted.

</td>
</tr>
<tr>
<td>

                S V   **O**
(d) The books were expensive. I bought | **them**. / ↓ / **which** **that**

        O   **S** **V**
(e) The books **which** *I bought* were expensive.
(f) The books **that** *I bought* were expensive.
(g) The books **Ø** *I bought* were expensive.

</td>
<td>

Which or **that** can be used as an object in an adjective clause, as in (e) and (f).

</td>
</tr>
<tr>
<td></td>
<td>

An object pronoun can be omitted from an adjective clause, as in (g). (e), (f) and (g) have the same meaning.

</td>
</tr>
</table>

A pyramid is a structure **that / which** is square at the bottom and has four sides that come together at the top in a point.

12-5 SINGULAR AND PLURAL VERBS IN ADJECTIVE CLAUSES

(a) I know **the man** *who **is** sitting over there.*	In (a): The verb in the adjective clause (**is**) is singular because **who** refers to a singular noun, "man."
(b) I know **the people** *who **are** sitting over there.*	In (b): The verb in the adjective clause (**are**) is plural because **who** refers to a plural noun, "people."

I know *a person* who **lives** on a boat.
I know *some people* who **live** on a boat.

12-6 USING PREPOSITIONS IN ADJECTIVE CLAUSES

PREP Obj. (a) The man was helpful. I talked **to** **him**.	**Whom**, **which**, and **that** can be used as the object of a preposition in an adjective clause. REMINDER: An object pronoun can be omitted from an adjective clause, as in (d) and (i).
Obj. **PREP** (b) The man **whom** *I talked **to*** was helpful. (c) The man **that** *I talked **to*** was helpful. (d) The man Ø *I talked **to*** was helpful. **PREP** **Obj.** (e) The man **to** **whom** *I talked* was helpful.	
	In very formal English, a preposition often comes at the beginning of an adjective clause, as in (e) and (j). The preposition is followed by either **whom** or **which** (not **that**) and the pronoun CANNOT be omitted.
PREP Obj. (f) The chair is hard. I am sitting **in** **it**.	(b), (c), (d), and (e) have the same meaning.
Obj. **PREP** (g) The chair **which** *I am sitting **in*** is hard. (h) The chair **that** *I am sitting **in*** is hard. (i) The chair Ø *I am sitting **in*** is hard. **PREP** **Obj.** (j) The chair **in** **which** *I am sitting* is hard.	(g), (h), (i), and (j) have the same meaning.

12-7 USING *WHOSE* IN ADJECTIVE CLAUSES

(a) The man called the police. **His car** → *whose car* was stolen.	**Whose*** shows possession. In (a): We can change **his car** to **whose car** to make an adjective clause.
(b) The man **whose car was stolen** called the police.	In (b): *whose car was stolen* = an adjective clause.
(c) I know a girl. **Her brother** → *whose brother* is a movie star.	In (c): We can change *her brother* to *whose brother* to make an adjective clause.
(d) I know a girl **whose brother** is a movie star.	
(e) The people were friendly. We bought **their house.** → *whose house*	In (e): We can change *their house* to *whose house* to make an adjective clause.
(f) The people **whose house we bought** were friendly.	

***Whose** and **who's** have the same pronunciation but NOT the same meaning.

Who's = **who is**: *Who's (who is) your teacher?*

Let me tell you about some of the people at this party.
There is the man **whose car** was stolen.
Over there is the woman **whose husband** you met yesterday.
There is the professor **whose course** I'm taking.

12-8 MORE PHRASAL VERBS (SEPARABLE)*

cross out	*draw a line through*
do over	*do again*
fill in	*complete a sentence by writing in a blank*
fill out	*write information in a form (e.g., an application form)*
fill up	*fill completely with gas, water, coffee, etc.*
find out	*discover information*
give up	*quit doing something or quit trying*
leave out	*omit*
start over	*start again*
tear down	*destroy a building*
tear off	*detach, tear along a dotted or perforated line*
tear out of	*remove a piece of paper from a book or notebook*
tear up	*tear into small pieces*

*See 9-8 and 9-9 for more information about phrasal verbs.

12-9 MORE PHRASAL VERBS (NONSEPARABLE)*

(a) Last night some friends **dropped in**.	In (a): **drop in** is not followed by an object.
(b) Let's **drop in on** *Alice* this afternoon. Let's **drop in on** *her* this afternoon.	In (b): **drop in on** is followed by an object.
	Some phrasal verbs are three-word verbs when they are followed by an object. These verbs are nonseparable.

drop in (on)	*visit without calling first or without an invitation*
drop out (of)	*stop attending (school)*
fool around (with)	*have fun while wasting time*
get along (with)	*have a good relationship with*
get back (from)	*return from (a trip)*
get through (with)	*finish*
grow up (in)	*become an adult*
look out (for)	*be careful*
run out (of)	*finish the supply of (something)*
watch out (for)	*be careful*

*See 9-8 and 9-9 for more information about phrasal verbs.

CHAPTER 13
Comparisons

13-1 MAKING COMPARISONS WITH *AS . . . AS*

(a) Tina is 21 years old. Sam is also 21. Tina is **as old as** Sam (is). (b) Mike came **as quickly as** he could.	**As . . . as** is used to say that the two parts of a comparison are equal or the same in some way. In (a): **as** + *adjective* + **as** In (b): **as** + *adverb* + **as**
(c) Ted is 20. Tina is 21. Ted is **not as old as** Tina. (d) Ted is**n't quite as** old **as** Tina. (e) Amy is 5. She is**n't nearly as** old **as** Tina.	Negative form: **not as . . . as**.* **Quite** and **nearly** are often used with the negative: In (d): **not quite as . . . as** = a small difference. In (e): **not nearly as . . . as** = a big difference.
(f) Sam is **just as old as** Tina. (g) Ted is **nearly/almost as** old **as** Tina.	Common modifiers of **as . . . as** are **just** (meaning "exactly") and **nearly/almost**.

*Also possible: **not so . . . as**: *Ted is **not so old as** Tina.*

13-2 COMPARATIVE AND SUPERLATIVE

(a) "A" is **older than** "B." (b) "A" and "B" are **older than** "C" and "D." (c) Ed is **more generous than** his brother.	The comparative compares "this/these" to "that/those." Form: **-er** or **more**. (See Chart 13-3.) NOTICE: A comparative is followed by **than**.
(d) "A", "B", "C", and "D" are sisters. "A" is **the oldest** *of all* four sisters. (e) A woman in Turkey claims to be **the oldest person** *in the world*. (f) Ed is **the most generous person** *in his family*.	The superlative compares one part of a whole group to all the rest of the group. Form: **-est** or **most**. (See Chart 13-3 for forms.) NOTICE: A superlative begins with **the**.

13-3 COMPARATIVE AND SUPERLATIVE FORMS OF ADJECTIVES AND ADVERBS

		COMPARATIVE	SUPERLATIVE	
ONE-SYLLABLE ADJECTIVES	old wise	older wiser	the oldest the wisest	For most one-syllable adjectives, **-er** and **-est** are added.
TWO-SYLLABLE ADJECTIVES	famous wise	more famous wiser	the most famous the wisest	For most two-syllable adjectives, **more** and **most** are used.
	busy pretty	busier prettier	the busiest the prettiest	**-Er/-est** are used with two-syllable adjectives that end in -y. The -y is changed to -i.
	clever gentle friendly	cleverer more clever gentler more gentle friendlier more friendly	the cleverest the most clever the gentlest the most gentle the friendliest the most friendly	Some two-syllable adjectives use **-er/-est** or **more/most**: *able, angry, clever, common, cruel, friendly, gentle, handsome, narrow, pleasant, polite, quiet, simple, sour.*
ADJECTIVES WITH THREE OR MORE SYLLABLES	important fascinating	more important more fascinating	the most important the most fascinating	**More** and **most** are used with long adjectives.
IRREGULAR ADJECTIVES	good bad	better worse	the best the worst	**Good** and **bad** have irregular comparative and superlative forms.
-LY ADVERBS	carefully slowly	more carefully more slowly	the most carefully the most slowly	**More** and **most** are used with adverbs that end in **-ly**.*
ONE-SYLLABLE ADVERBS	fast hard	faster harder	the fastest the hardest	The **-er** and **-est** forms are used with one-syllable adverbs.
IRREGULAR ADVERBS	well badly far	better worse farther/further**	the best the worst the farthest/furthest	

*Exception: **early** is both an adjective and an adverb. Forms: *earlier, earliest.*

Both **farther and **further** are used to compare physical distances: *I walked farther/further than my friend did.* **Further** (but not **farther**) can also mean "additional": *I need further information.*

13-4 USING COMPARATIVES

(a) I'm older *than **my brother*** (*is*). (b) I'm older *than **he*** *is*. (c) I'm older *than **him***. (*informal*)	In formal English, a subject pronoun (e.g., *he*) follows ***than***, as in (b). In everday, informal spoken English, an object pronoun (e.g., *him*) often follows ***than***, as in (c).
(d) He works harder *than **I do***. (e) I arrived earlier *than they **did***.	Frequently an auxiliary verb follows the subject after ***than***. In (d): *than I do = than I work*.
(f) Tom is ***much/a lot/far*** older than I am. INCORRECT: Tom is very older than I am. (g) Ann drives ***much/a lot/far*** more carefully than she used to. (h) Ben is ***a little*** (***bit***) older than me.	***Very*** often modifies adjectives and adverbs: e.g., *Tom is very old. He drives very carefully.* However, ***very*** is NOT used to modify comparative adjectives and adverbs. Instead, they are often modified by ***much***, ***a lot***, or ***far***, as in (f) and (g). Another common modifier is ***a little/a little bit***, as in (h).
(i) A pen is ***less expensive than*** a book. (j) A pen is ***not as expensive as*** a book. (k) A pen is *not as large as* a book. INCORRECT: A pen is less large than a book.	The opposite of ***-er/more*** is expressed by ***less*** or ***not as . . . as***. (i) and (j) have the same meaning. ***Less*** (***not as . . . as***) is used with adjectives and adverbs of **more than one syllable**. Only ***not as . . . as*** (NOT ***less***) is used with one-syllable adjectives or adverbs, as in (k).

Ted is out of shape. I can run a lot faster and farther *than he **can**.*

13-5 USING *MORE* WITH NOUNS

(a) Would you like some *more coffee*? (b) Not everyone is here. I expect *more people* to come later.	In (a): "coffee" is a noun. When *more* is used with nouns, it often has the meaning of *additional*. It is not necessary to use *than*.
(c) There are *more people* in China *than* there are in the United States.	*More* is also used with nouns to make complete comparisons by using *than*.
(d) Do you have enough coffee, or would you like some *more*?	When the meaning is clear, the noun may be omitted and *more* used by itself.

13-6 REPEATING A COMPARATIVE

(a) Because he was afraid, he walked *faster and faster*. (b) Life in the modern world is becoming *more and more complex*.	Repeating a comparative gives the idea that something becomes progressively greater, i.e., it increases in intensity, quality, or quantity.

As I continued to row the boat, my arms got *weaker and weaker* until I had almost no strength left in them at all.

13-7 USING DOUBLE COMPARATIVES

(a) **The harder** you study, **the more** you will learn. (b) **The older** he got, **the quieter** he became. (c) **The more** she studied, **the more** she learned. (d) **The warmer** the weather (is), **the better** I like it.	A double comparative has two parts; both parts begin with *the*, as in the examples. The second part of the comparison is the **result** of the first part. In (a): If you study harder, the result will be that you will learn more.
(e) A: Should we ask Jenny and Jim to the party too? B: Why not? **The more, the merrier**. (f) A: When should we leave? B: **The sooner, the better**.	**The more, the merrier** and **the sooner, the better** are two common expressions. In (e): It is good to have more people at the party. In (f): It is good if we leave as soon as we can.

13-8 USING SUPERLATIVES

(a) Tokyo is one of **the largest cities in the world**. (b) David is **the most generous person I have ever known**. (c) I have three books. These two are quite good, but this one is the **best** (book) **of all**.	Typical completions when a superlative is used: In (a): superlative + *in a place* (*the world, this class, my family, the corporation,* etc.) In (b): superlative + adjective clause. In (c): superlative + *of all*.
(d) I took four final exams. The final in accounting was **the least difficult** of all.	*The least* has the opposite meaning of *the most*.

Waterfalls of the World

Angel Falls is **the highest** waterfall in the world.

Niagara Falls
United States and Canada
53 meters

Giessbach Falls
Switzerland
604 meters

Cuquenán Falls
Venezuela
610 meters

Angel Falls
Venezuela
807 meters

13-9 USING *THE SAME, SIMILAR, DIFFERENT, LIKE, ALIKE*

(a) John and Mary have **the same books**. (b) John and Mary have **similar books**. (c) John and Mary have **different books**. (d) Their books are **the same**. (e) Their books are **similar**. (f) Their books are **different**.	**The same**, **similar**, and **different** are used as adjectives. Notice: **the** always precedes **same**.

(g) This book is **the same as** that one.
 (h) This book is **similar to** that one.
 (i) This book is **different from** that one.
	Notice: **the same** is followed by **as**;
	        similar is followed by **to**;
	        different is followed by **from**.*

(j) She is **the same age as** my mother. My shoes are **the same size as** yours.	A noun may come between **the same** and **as**, as in (j).

(k) My pen **is like** your pen.
 (l) My pen and your pen **are alike**.
	Notice in (k) and (l):
	    noun + **be like** + *noun*
	    noun and *noun* + **be alike**

(m) She **looks like** her sister.
     It **looks like** rain.
     It **sounds like** thunder.
     This material **feels like** silk.
     That **smells like** gas.
     This chemical **tastes like** salt.
     Stop **acting like** a fool.
     He **seems like** a nice fellow.
	In addition to following **be**, **like** also follows certain verbs, primarily those dealing with the senses. Notice the examples in (m).

(n) The twins **look alike**.
     We **think alike**.
     Most four-year-olds **act alike**.
     My sister and I **talk alike**.
     The little boys **are dressed alike**.
	Alike may follow a few verbs other than **be**. Notice the examples in (n).

*In informal speech, native speakers might use **than** instead of **from** after **different**. **From** is considered correct in formal English, unless the comparison is completed by a clause: *I have a different attitude now than I used to have.*

CHAPTER *14*
Noun Clauses

14-1 NOUN CLAUSES: INTRODUCTION

(a) $\overset{\text{S}}{\text{I}}\ \overset{\text{V}}{\text{know}}\ \overset{\text{O}}{\textbf{his address}}$.
(noun phrase)
	Verbs are often followed by objects. The object is usually a noun phrase,* as in (a):
	    his address is a noun phrase;
	    his address is the object of the verb *know*.

(b) $\overset{\text{S}}{\text{I}}\ \overset{\text{V}}{\text{know}}\ \overset{\text{O}}{\textbf{where he lives}}$. *(noun clause)*	Some verbs can be followed by noun clauses.* In (b): ***where he lives*** is a noun clause; ***where he lives*** is the object of the verb *know*.
(c) I know **where he lives**.	A noun clause has its own subject and verb. In (c): ***he*** is the subject of the noun clause; ***lives*** is the verb of the noun clause.
(d) I know **where he lives**. *(noun clause)*	A noun clause can begin with a question word. (See 14-2.)
(e) I don't know **if he is married**. *(noun clause)*	A noun clause can begin with *if* or **whether**. (See 14-4.)
(f) I know **that the world is round**. *(noun clause)*	A noun clause can begin with **that**. (See 14-5.)

*Grammar terminology:

    A **phrase** is a group of related words. It does not contain a subject and a verb.

    A **clause** is a group of related words. It contains a subject and a verb.

A noun clause is a dependent clause and cannot stand alone as a sentence. It must be connected to an independent clause (a main clause).

14-2 NOUN CLAUSES THAT BEGIN WITH A QUESTION WORD

The following question words can be used to introduce a noun clause: **when, where, why, how, who, whom, what, which, whose.**

INFORMATION QUESTIONS	NOUN CLAUSES	Notice in the examples: Question word order is NOT used in a noun clause.
Where **does he live**?	(a) I don't know *where* **he lives**.	INCORRECT: *I know where does he live.*
When **did they leave**?	(b) Do you know *when* **they left**?	CORRECT: *I know where he lives.*
What **did she say**?	(c) Please tell me *what* **she said**.	
Why **is Tom** absent?	(d) I wonder *why* **Tom is** absent.	

When *was the first wheel* invented?
Do you know when *the first wheel was* invented?

14-3 NOUN CLAUSES WITH *WHO, WHAT, WHOSE + BE*

QUESTION	NOUN CLAUSE	A noun or pronoun that follows main verb *be* in a question comes in front of *be* in a noun clause, as in (a) and (b). A prepositional phrase (e.g., *in the office*) does NOT come in front of *be* in a noun clause, as in (c) and (d).
Who **is** **that boy**?	(a) I don't know who **that boy** **is**.	
Whose pen **is** **this**?	(b) I don't know whose pen **this** **is**.	
Who **is** in the office?	(c) I don't know **who** **is** in the office.	
Whose pen **is** on the desk?	(d) I don't know **whose pen** **is** on the desk.	

14-4 NOUN CLAUSES WHICH BEGIN WITH *IF* OR *WHETHER**

YES/NO QUESTION	NOUN CLAUSE	When a yes/no question is changed to a noun clause, *if* is usually used to introduce the clause.
Is Eric at home? Does the bus stop here? Did Alice go to Chicago?	$\underbrace{\text{S}}\ \underbrace{\text{V}}\ \underbrace{\text{O}}$ (a) I don't know *if Eric is at home*. (b) Do you know *if the bus stops here*? (c) I wonder *if Alice went to Chicago*.	
(d) I don't know *if Eric is at home or not*.		When *if* introduces a noun clause, the expression *or not* may come at the end of the clause, as in (d).
(e) I don't know *whether Eric is at home*. (f) I don't know *whether Eric is at home or not*. (g) I don't know *whether or not Eric is at home*.		In (e): *whether* has the same meaning as *if*. In (f): *or not* can come at the end of the noun clause. In (g): *or not* can come immediately after *whether*. (NOTE: *or not* cannot come immediately after *if*.)

*See Chart 15-5 for the use of *if* and *whether* with *ask* in reported speech.

I wonder ***whether prople can communicate with dolphins***.
Do you know ***if scientists have learned how to talk with dolphins?***

14-5 NOUN CLAUSES WHICH BEGIN WITH *THAT*

<table>
<tr>
<td>

   S   V   O
(a) ⌐I⌐ ⌐think⌐ **that** *Mr. Jones is a good teacher.*

(b) I hope **that** *you can come to the game.*
(c) Mary realizes **that** *she should study harder.*
(d) I dreamed **that** *I was on the top of a mountain.*

</td>
<td>

A noun clause can be introduced by the word **that**.
In (a): *that Mr. Jones is a good teacher* is a noun clause. It is the object of the verb *think*.
"*That*-clauses" are frequently used as the objects of verbs which express mental activity. (See the list below.)

</td>
</tr>
<tr>
<td>

(e) I think **that** *Mr. Jones is a good teacher.*
(f) I think Ø *Mr. Jones is a good teacher.*

</td>
<td>

The word **that** is often omitted, especially in speaking. (e) and (f) have the same meaning.

</td>
</tr>
</table>

COMMON VERBS FOLLOWED BY "*THAT*-CLAUSES"★

assume that	*guess that*	*learn that*	*realize that*
believe that	*hear that*	*notice that*	*suppose that*
discover that	*hope that*	*predict that*	*suspect that*
dream that	*know that*	*prove that*	*think that*

★The verbs in the above list are those that are emphasized in the exercises. Some other common verbs that can be followed by "*that*-clauses" are:

agree that	*fear that*	*imagine that*	*read that*	*reveal that*
conclude that	*feel that*	*indicate that*	*recall that*	*show that*
decide that	*figure out that*	*observe that*	*recognize that*	*teach that*
demonstrate that	*find out that*	*presume that*	*regret that*	*understand that*
doubt that	*forget that*	*pretend that*	*remember that*	

A: Do you believe **that** a monster really exists in Loch Ness in Scotland?

B: I don't know. Look at this story in the newspaper. It says **that** *some scientists have proved* **that** *the Loch Ness Monster exists.*

A: You shouldn't always believe what you read in the newspapers. I think **that** *the monster is purely fictional.*

14-6 SUBSTITUTING *SO* FOR A *"THAT*-CLAUSE" IN CONVERSATIONAL RESPONSES

(a) A: Is Pedro from Mexico? B: **I think so.** *(I think that Pedro is from Mexico.)* (b) A: Does Judy live in Dallas? B: **I believe so.** *(I believe that Judy lives in Dallas.)* (c) A: Did you pass the test? B: **I hope so.** *(I hope that I passed the test.)*	*Think, believe*, and **hope** are frequently followed by **so** in conversational English in response to a yes/no question. They are alternatives to answering *yes, no*, or *I don't know*.★
	So replaces a "*that*-clause." In (a): *so = that Pedro is from Mexico.*
(d) A: Is Ali at home? B: **I don't think so.** *(I don't think that Ali is at home.)* (e) A: Is Jack married? B: **I don't believe so.** *(I don't believe that Jack is married.)*	Negative usage of **think so** and **believe so**: 　　　*I don't think so.* 　　　*I don't believe so.*
(f) A: Did you fail the test? B: **I hope not.** *(I hope that I didn't fail the test.)*	Negative usage of **hope** in conversational responses: *I hope not.*

★In addition to expressions with ***think, believe,*** and ***hope,*** the following expressions are commonly used in conversational responses: *I guess so, I guess not, I suppose so, I suppose not, I'm afraid so, I'm afraid not.*

14-7 OTHER USES OF "*THAT*-CLAUSES"

(a) I'm **sure that** the bus stops here. (b) I'm **glad that** you're feeling better today. (c) I'm **sorry that** I missed class yesterday. (d) I **was disappointed that** the peace conference failed.	"*That*-clauses" can follow certain expressions with **be** + *adjective* or **be** + *past participle*. The word "*that*" can be omitted with no change in meaning: *I'm sure Ø the bus stops here.*
(e) **It is true that** the world is round. (f) **It is a fact that** the world is round.	Two very common expressions followed by "*that*-clauses" are: *it is true (that)* and *it is a fact (that)*

COMMON EXPRESSIONS FOLLOWED BY "*THAT*-CLAUSES"★

be afraid that	*be disappointed that*	*be sorry that*	*It is true that . . .*
be aware that	*be glad that*	*be sure that*	*It is a fact that . . .*
be certain that	*be happy that*	*be surprised that*	
be convinced that	*be pleased that*	*be worried that*	

★The above list contains expressions emphasized in the exercises. Some other common expressions with **be** that are frequently followed by "*that*-clauses" are:

be amazed that	*be delighted that*	*be impressed that*	*be sad that*
be angry that	*be fortunate that*	*be lucky that*	*be shocked that*
be ashamed that	*be furious that*	*be positive that*	*be terrified that*
be astounded that	*be horrified that*	*be proud that*	*be thrilled that*

CHAPTER **15**

Quoted Speech and Reported Speech

15-1 QUOTED SPEECH

Sometimes we want to quote a speaker's words—to write a speaker's exact words. Exact quotations are used in many kinds of writing, such as newspaper articles, stories and novels, and academic papers. When we quote a speaker's words, we use quotation marks.

SPEAKER:	SPEAKER'S EXACT WORDS	QUOTING THE SPEAKER'S WORDS
Jane:	*Cats are fun to watch.*	(a) Jane said, **"Cats are fun to watch."**
Mike:	*Yes, I agree. They're graceful and playful. Do you own a cat?*	(b) Mike said, **"Yes, I agree. They're graceful and playful. Do you own a cat?"**

HOW TO WRITE QUOTATIONS:

1. Put a comma after *said.** ──────────► Jane said,
2. Put quotation marks. ──────────► Jane said, "
3. Capitalize the first word of the quotation. ──────► Jane said, "C
4. Write the quotation. Put a final period. ──────► Jane said, "Cats are fun to watch.
5. Put quotation marks *after* the period. ──────► Jane said, "Cats are fun to watch."

6. When there are two (or more) sentences in a quotation, put the quotation marks at the beginning and end of the whole quote. Do not put quotation marks around each sentence.	Mike said, **"Yes, I agree. They're graceful and playful. Do you own a cat?"**
7. As with a period, put the quotation marks after a question mark at the end of a quote.	INCORRECT: Mike said, **"Yes, I agree." "They're graceful and playful." "Do you own a cat"?**

8. Be sure to put quotation marks above the line, not on the line.

INCORRECT: *Ann said, „ My book is on the table.„,*

CORRECT: *Ann said, " My book is on the table."*

*Other common verbs besides *say* that introduce quotations: *admit, announce, answer, ask, complain, explain, inquire, report, reply, shout, state, write.*

15-2 QUOTED SPEECH vs. REPORTED SPEECH*

QUOTED SPEECH:	*Quoted speech* refers to reproducing another person's exact words. Quotation marks are used.
REPORTED SPEECH:	*Reported speech* refers to reproducing the idea of another person's words. Not all of the exact words are used: verb forms and pronouns may change. Quotation marks are not used.

QUOTED SPEECH	REPORTED SPEECH	Notice in the examples:
(a) Ann said, **"I am hungry."**	(b) Ann said **that she was hungry.**	The verb forms and pronouns change from quoted speech to reported speech.
(c) Tom said, **"I need my pen."**	(d) Tom said **that he needed his pen**.	

*Quoted speech is also called *direct speech*. *Reported speech* is also called *indirect speech*.

15-3 VERB FORM USAGE IN REPORTED SPEECH: FORMAL SEQUENCE OF TENSES

FORMAL: If the main verb of the sentence is in the past (e.g., *said*), the verb in the noun clause is usually also in a past form.* Notice the verb form changes in the examples below.

QUOTED SPEECH	REPORTED SPEECH
(a) He said, "I *work* hard." ⟶	He said (that) he *worked* hard.
(b) He said, "I *am working* hard." ⟶	He said (that) he *was working* hard.
(c) He said, "I *have worked* hard." ⟶	He said (that) he *had worked* hard.
(d) He said, "I *worked* hard." ⟶	He said (that) he *had worked* hard.
(e) He said, "I *am going to work* hard." ⟶	He said (that) he *was going to work* hard.
(f) He said, "I *will work* hard." ⟶	He said (that) he *would work* hard.
(g) He said, "I *can work* hard." ⟶	He said (that) he *could work* hard.
(h) He said, "I *may work* hard." ⟶	He said (that) he *might work* hard.
(i) He said, "I *have to work* hard." ⟶	He said (that) he *had to work* hard.
(j) He said, "I *must work* hard." ⟶	He said (that) he *had to work* hard.
(k) He said, "I *should work* hard." ⟶	He said (that) he *should work* hard. (*no change*)
(l) He said, "I *ought to work* hard." ⟶	He said (that) he *ought to work* hard. (*no change*)

INFORMAL: Sometimes, especially in speaking, the verb in the noun clause is not changed if the speaker is reporting something *immediately* or *soon after* it was said.

(m) Immediate reporting:	A: What did Ann just say? I didn't hear her. B: She *said* (that) she *is* hungry.
(n) Later reporting:	A: What did Ann say when she got home last night? B: She *said* (that) she *was* hungry.

*If the main verb of the sentence is in the present (e.g., *says*), no change is made in the verb tense or modal in the noun clause.

He says, "I *work* hard." ⟶ He says (that) he *works* hard.
He says, "I*'m working* hard." ⟶ He says (that) he*'s working* hard.
He says, "I *worked* hard." ⟶ He says (that) he *worked* hard.
He says, "I *will work* hard." ⟶ He says (that) he *will work* hard.

15-4   USING *SAY* vs. *TELL*

(a) Ann *said that* she was hungry.	***Say*** is followed immediately by a noun clause.
(b) Ann **told me** *that* she was hungry. (c) Ann **told us** *that* she was hungry. (d) Ann **told John** *that* she was hungry. (e) Ann **told someone** *that* she was hungry.	***Tell*** is NOT followed immediately by a noun clause. ***Tell*** is followed immediately by a (pro)noun object (e.g., *me, us, John, someone*) and then by a noun clause. INCORRECT: Ann told that she was hungry.

15-5   USING *ASK IF*

Ask, NOT **say** or ***tell***, is used to report yes/no questions.	
YES/NO QUESTION Sam said to me, *"Are you hungry?"* Sam said to Jane, *"Are you hungry?"*	**NOUN CLAUSE** (a) Sam **asked** me *if* I was hungry. (b) Sam **asked** Jane *if* she was hungry.
(c) INCORRECT: Sam asked me that I was hungry.	***If***, NOT ***that***, is used after **ask** to introduce a noun clause.
(d) Sam *asked* me **if** I was hungry. (e) Sam *asked* me **whether** I was hungry.	***Whether*** has the same meaning as ***if***. (See Chart 14-4 for the use of ***or not***.)
(f) Sam *asked* **if** I was hungry.	The (pro)noun object (e.g., *me*) may be omitted after **ask**.
(g) Sam **wanted to know if** I was hungry. (h) Sam **wondered if** I was hungry. (i) Sam **inquired whether** or not I was hungry.	In addition to **ask**, yes/no questions can be reported by using **want to know**, **wonder**, and **inquire**.

Alex **asked** Susan *if she smelled smoke.*

15-6 USING VERB + INFINITIVE TO REPORT SPEECH

<table>
<tr><td colspan="2">QUOTED SPEECH</td><td>REPORTED SPEECH</td></tr>
<tr><td colspan="2">(a) Joe said, "Please come to my party."
(b) Joe said, "Can you come to my party?"
(c) Joe said, "Would you like to come to my party?"</td><td>(d) Joe invited me to come to his party.</td></tr>
</table>

			Some verbs are followed immediately by a (pro)noun object and then an infinitive phrase. These verbs (see the list below) are often used to report speech.

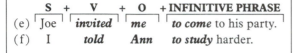

	S	**V**	**O**	**+ INFINITIVE PHRASE**
(e)	Joe	*invited*	*me*	*to come* to his party.
(f)	I	*told*	*Ann*	*to study* harder.

REPORTING SPEECH: VERB + (PRO)NOUN OBJECT + INFINITIVE★

advise someone to	*invite someone to*	*remind someone to*
ask someone to	*order someone to*	*tell someone to*
encourage someone to	*permit someone to*	*warn someone to*

★Other common verbs followed by a (pro)noun object and an infinitive:
allow, beg, challenge, convince, direct, expect, instruct, persuade, urge

15-7 SOME TROUBLESOME VERBS: *ADVISE, SUGGEST,* AND *RECOMMEND*

(a) Ed *advised me* **to call** a doctor. (b) Ed *advised* **calling** a doctor.	(a) and (b) have the same meaning. In (a): When **advise** is followed by a (pro)noun object, an infinitive is used. In (b): When there is no (pro)noun object after **advise**, a gerund is used.
(c) Ed *suggested* **calling** a doctor. (d) Ed *recommended* **calling** a doctor.	**Suggest** and **recommend** can also be followed immediately by a gerund.

(e)   CORRECT: Ed **suggested that I should call** a doctor.
    INCORRECT: Ed suggested me to call a doctor.
(f)   CORRECT: Ed **recommended that I should call** a doctor.
    INCORRECT: Ed recommended me to call a doctor.
	Suggest and **recommend** cannot be followed by a (pro)noun object and an infinitive, but they can be followed by a "*that*-clause" in which **should** is used.★

★The use of **should** in the noun clause is not necessary. However, if **should** is not used, the verb in the noun clause is always in the simple form after *suggest* and *recommend*:

Ed **suggested/recommended** that
{
I call a doctor. (not *called*)
we call a doctor. (not *called*)
Ann call a doctor. (not *calls* or *called*)
he call a doctor. (not *calls* or *called*)

CHAPTER 16
Using Wish; *Using* If

16-1 EXPRESSING WISHES ABOUT THE PRESENT/FUTURE

<table>
<tr><th>THE TRUE SITUATION</th><th>EXPRESSING A WISH ABOUT THAT SITUATION</th><th rowspan="5">People often make wishes when they want reality to be different, to be exactly the opposite of (contrary to) the true situation.

A noun clause* usually follows wish. Special verb forms are used in the noun clause. When a speaker expresses a wish about a present situation, s/he uses a past verb form.</th></tr>
<tr><td>I don't know how to dance.</td><td>(a) I wish (that) I knew how to dance.</td></tr>
<tr><td>I don't have a bicycle.</td><td>(b) I wish I had a bicycle.</td></tr>
<tr><td>Ron has to work tonight.</td><td>(c) Ron wishes he didn't have to work tonight.</td></tr>
<tr><td>I can't speak Chinese.</td><td>(d) I wish I could speak Chinese.</td></tr>
<tr><td>I'm not home in bed.
Ann isn't home in bed.
It's cold today.
We aren't in Hawaii.</td><td>(e) I wish I were home in bed.
(f) Ann wishes she were home in bed.
(g) I wish it weren't cold today.
(h) We wish we were in Hawaii.</td><td>Notice in (e), (f), (g), and (h): were is used for all subjects:

I wish { I / you / he / she / it / we / they } were . . . .</td></tr>
</table>

*For more information about noun clauses which begin with ***that,*** see Chapter 14.

16-2 EXPRESSING WISHES ABOUT THE PAST

The PAST PERFECT* is used after **wish** when people make wishes about a past situation.	
THE TRUE SITUATION	**MAKING A WISH ABOUT THE PAST**
I *didn't study* for the test.	(a) *I wish* (that) I **had studied** for the test.
Jim *didn't finish* his work.	(b) *Jim wishes* he **had finished** his work.
I *went* to the meeting.	(c) *I wish* I **hadn't gone** to the meeting.

*See Chart 7-10 for the forms of the past perfect.

WISH ABOUT THE PRESENT: Linda wishes she **didn't have to clean** up the kitchen this morning.

WISH ABOUT THE PAST: Linda wishes her roommate **had washed** the dishes last night.

16-3   USING *IF*: CONTRARY-TO-FACT IN THE PRESENT/FUTURE

If is often used to talk about situations that are contrary to fact, i.e., situations that are the opposite of the true situation.	

TRUE SITUATION: (a) I *don't have* enough money.
MAKING A WISH: (b) I wish I *had* enough money.
USING *IF*: (c) If I *had* enough money, I *would buy* a car.
　　　　　　　(d) If I *had* enough money, I *could buy* a car.

TRUE SITUATION: (e) The weather *isn't* nice today.
MAKING A WISH: (f) I wish the weather *were* nice today.
USING *IF*: (g) If the weather *were* nice today, I *would go* to the park.
　　　　　　　(h) If the weather *were* nice today, I *could go* to the park.

Contrary-to-fact sentences with an "*if*-clause" and a "result clause" are called *conditional sentences*. Special verb forms are used. The SIMPLE PAST TENSE is used to discuss a present or future situation in an "*if*-clause." *Would* or *could* is used in the result clause.
　　　　IF-CLAUSE: simple past tense　　RESULT CLAUSE: *would*/*could* + simple form

⎧ *if*-clause ⎫　⎧ result clause ⎫ (i) ⎩If I *had* enough money,⎭ ⎩I *would buy* a car.⎭ ⎧ result clause ⎫　⎧ *if*-clause ⎫ (j) ⎩I *would go* to the park⎭ ⎩if the weather *were* nice.⎭	In (i) and (j), the speakers are talking about present/future situations, but they use the simple past in the "*if*-clause."★
(k) If I had enough money, I *would* buy a car. 　　(*The speaker wants to buy a car.*) (l) If I had enough money, I *could* buy a car. 　　(*The speaker is expressing a possibility*.)	*Would* expresses intended or desired results. *Could* expresses possible options. *Could* = *would be able to*.
(m) If the *weather were* nice, I'd go to the park. (n) If *Kate were* here, she would help us. (o) If *I were* you, I wouldn't accept that job.	Notice in (m), (n), and (o): *were* (instead of *was*) is usually used for singular subjects in a contrary-to-fact "*if*-clause."

★An "*if*-clause" is a kind of adverb clause. See Chart 9-6.

16-4 USING *IF*: TRUE vs. CONTRARY-TO-FACT IN THE PRESENT/FUTURE

TRUE SITUATION: (a) If you **need** some money, I $\left\{\begin{array}{l} will \\ can \end{array}\right\}$ **lend** you some. *(simple present)* **CONTRARY-TO-FACT SITUATION:** (b) If you **needed** some money, I $\left\{\begin{array}{l} would \\ could \end{array}\right\}$ **lend** you some. *(simple past)*	In (a): Perhaps you need some money. If that is true, I will (or can) lend you some. Reminder: Do not use **will** in an "*if*-clause." (See Chart 3-5.) In (b): In truth, you don't need any money. But if the opposite were true, I would (or could) lend you some.

VERB FORM USAGE SUMMARY (PRESENT/FUTURE)

SITUATION:	*IF*-CLAUSE:	RESULT CLAUSE:
TRUE	**simple present**	$\left\{\begin{array}{l} will \\ can \end{array}\right\}$ + **simple form**
CONTRARY-TO-FACT	**simple past**	$\left\{\begin{array}{l} would \\ could \end{array}\right\}$ + **simple form**

16-5   USING *IF*: CONTRARY-TO-FACT IN THE PAST

Conditional sentences that discuss past time have special verb forms: 　*If*-CLAUSE: **the past perfect**　RESULT CLAUSE: *would have/could have* + **past participle**
TRUE SITUATION: (a) I *didn't have* enough money. MAKING A WISH: (b) I wish I *had had* enough money. 　　USING **IF**: (c) If I **had had** enough money, I **would have bought** a car. 　　　　　(d) If I **had had** enough money, I **could have bought** a car. TRUE SITUATION: (e) The weather *wasn't* nice yesterday. MAKING A WISH: (f) I wish the weather *had been* nice yesterday. 　　USING **IF**: (g) If the weather **had been** nice yesterday, I **would have gone** to the park. 　　　　　(h) If the weather **had been** nice yesterday, I **could have gone** to the park.

16-6 SUMMARY: VERB FORMS IN SENTENCES WITH *IF* (CONDITIONAL SENTENCES)

SITUATION	*IF*-CLAUSE	RESULT CLAUSE	EXAMPLES
TRUE IN THE PRESENT/FUTURE	simple present	*will* *can* } + simple form	If I *have* enough money, I { *will buy* *can buy* } a ticket.
CONTRARY-TO-FACT IN THE PRESENT/FUTURE	simple past	*would* *could* } + simple form	If I *had* enough money, I { *would buy* *could buy* } a ticket.
CONTRARY-TO-FACT IN THE PAST	past perfect	*would have* *could have* } + past participle	If I *had had* enough money, I { *would have bought* *could have bought* } a ticket.

Sam *had* an automobile accident yesterday because a squirrel *ran* in front of his car.

Sam **would not have had** an accident yesterday if a squirrel **had not run** in front of his car.

APPENDIX *1*

Preposition Combinations

A   *be* absent from
    be accustomed to
        add *(this)* to *(that)*
    be acquainted with
        admire *(someone)* for *(something)*
    be afraid of
        agree with *(someone)* about/on *(something)*
    be angry at/with
        apologize to *(someone)* for *(something)*
        apply to *(a place)* for *(something)*
        approve of
        argue with *(someone)* about *(something)*
        arrive at *(a building, a room)*
        arrive in *(a city, a country)*
        ask *(someone)* about *(something)*
        ask *(someone)* for *(something)*
    be aware of

B   *be* bad for
        believe in
        belong to
    be bored with/by
        borrow *(something)* from *(someone)*

C   *be* clear to
        compare *(this)* to/with *(that)*
        complain to *(someone)* about *(something)*
    be composed of
        concentrate on
        consist of
    be crazy about
    be crowded with

D   depend on/upon *(someone)* for *(something)*
    be dependent on/upon *(someone)* for *(something)*
    be devoted to

be different from
    disagree with *(someone)* about *(something)*
be disappointed in
    discuss *(something)* with *(someone)*
    divide *(this)* into *(that)*
be divorced from
be done with
    dream about/of

E   *be* engaged to
    be equal to
    escape from
   be excited about
    excuse *(someone)* for *(something)*
   be exhausted from

F   *be* familiar with
   be famous for
   be finished with
    forgive *(someone)* for *(something)*
   be friendly to/with
   be frightened of/by
   be full of

G   get rid of
   be gone from
   be good for
    graduate from

H   happen to
    hear about/of
    hear from
    help *(someone)* with *(something)*
    hide *(something)* from *(someone)*
    hope for
   be hungry for

I   insist on
   be interested in
    introduce *(someone)* to *(someone)*
    invite *(someone)* to *(something)*
   be involved in

K *be* kind to
    know about

L   laugh at
    listen to
    look at
    look for
    look forward to

M *be* mad at
    be made of
    be married to
       matter to
    be the matter with
       multiply *(this)* by *(that)*

N *be* nice to

O *be* opposed to

P   pay for
    be patient with
    be pleased with
       point at
    be polite to
    be prepared for
       protect *(this)* from *(that)*
    be proud of

Q *be* qualified for

R *be* ready for
    be related to
       rely on/upon
    be responsible for

S *be* satisfied with
    be scared of/by
       search for
       separate *(this)* from *(that)*
    be similar to
    be sorry about *(something)*
    be sorry for *(someone)*
       speak to/with *(someone)* about *(something)*
       stare at
       subtract *(this)* from *(that)*
    be sure of

T   take care of
       talk to/with *(someone)* about *(something)*
       tell *(someone)* about *(something)*
    be terrified of/by
       thank *(someone)* for *(something)*
    be thirsty for
    be tired from
    be tired of
       travel to

W   wait for
       wait on
    be worried about

APPENDIX *2*
Phrasal Verbs

This list contains only those phrasal verbs used in the exercises in the text. The verbs with an asterisk (*) are nonseparable. The others are separable. See Charts 9-8 and 9-9 for a discussion of separable and nonseparable phrasal verbs.

A ask out . . . . *ask someone to go on a date*
C call back . . . . *return a telephone call*
   call off . . . . *cancel*
   *call on . . . . *ask to speak in class*
   call up . . . . *make a telephone call*
   cross out . . . . *draw a line through*
D do over . . . . *do again*
   *drop in (on) . . . . *visit without calling first or without an invitation*
   *drop out (of) . . . . *stop attending school*
F figure out . . . . *find the solution to a problem*
   fill in . . . . *complete a sentence by writing in a blank*
   fill out . . . . *write information in a form (e.g., an application form)*
   fill up . . . . *fill completely with gas, water, coffee, etc.*
   find out . . . . *discover information*
   *fool around (with) . . . . . *have fun while wasting time*
G *get along (with) . . . . *have a good relationship with*
   *get back (from) . . . . *return from a trip*
   *get in . . . . *enter a car, a taxi*
   *get off . . . . *leave a bus, an airplane, a train, a subway, a bicycle*
   *get on . . . . *enter a bus, an airplane, a train, a subway, a bicycle*
   *get out (of) . . . . *leave a car, a taxi*
   *get over . . . . *recover from an illness*
   *get through (with) . . . . . *finish*
   give back . . . . *return something to someone*
   give up . . . . *quit doing something or quit trying*
   *grow up (in) . . . . *become an adult*

H hand in . . . . *give homework, test papers, etc., to a teacher*

hand out . . . . *give something to this person, then that person, then another person, etc.*

hang up . . . . *(1) hang on a hanger or a hook; (2) end a telephone call*

K *keep on . . . . *continue*

L leave out . . . . *omit*

*look out (for) . . . . *be careful*

look up . . . . *look for information in a reference book*

M make up . . . . *invent*

P pay back . . . . *return money to someone*

pick up . . . . *lift*

put away . . . . *put something in its usual or proper place*

put back . . . . *return something to its original place*

put down . . . . *stop holding or carrying*

put off . . . . *postpone*

R *run into . . . . *meet by chance*

*run out (of) . . . . *finish the supply of something*

S shut off . . . . *stop a machine or light, turn off*

start over . . . . *start again*

T take off . . . . *remove clothes from one's body*

tear down . . . . *destroy a building*

tear off . . . . *detach, tear along a dotted or perforated line*

tear out (of) . . . . *remove a piece of paper from a book or notebook*

tear up . . . . *tear into small pieces*

throw away/out . . . . *put in the trash, discard*

try on . . . . *put on clothing to see if it fits*

turn down . . . . *decrease the volume*

turn off . . . . *stop a machine or a light, shut off*

turn on . . . . *start a machine or a light*

turn up . . . . *increase the volume*

W wake up . . . . *stop sleeping*

*watch out (for) . . . . *be careful*

write down . . . . *write a note on a piece of paper*

APPENDIX **3**

Guide for Correcting Writing Errors

To the student: Each number represents an area of usage. Your teacher will use these numbers when marking your writing to indicate that you have made an error. Refer to this list to find out what kind of error you have made and then make the necessary correction.

①   **SINGULAR-PLURAL**
     ① He have been here for six ① month.
     He has been here for six months.

②   **WORD FORM**
     ② I saw a beauty picture.
     I saw a beautiful picture.

③   **WORD CHOICE**
     ③ She got on the taxi.
     She got into the taxi.

④   **VERB TENSE**
     ④ He is here since June.
     He has been here since June.

⑤+   **ADD A WORD**
     ⑤+ I want ∧ go to the zoo.
     I want to go to the zoo.

⑤–   **OMIT A WORD**
     ⑤– She entered to the university.
     She entered the university.

⑥   **WORD ORDER**
     ⑥ I saw five times that movie.
     I saw that movie five times.

<table>
<tr><td>⑦</td><td>INCOMPLETE SENTENCE</td><td>⑦
I went to bed. Because I was tired.
I went to bed because I was tired.</td></tr>
<tr><td>⑧</td><td>SPELLING</td><td>⑧
An accident occured.
An accident occurred.</td></tr>
<tr><td>⑨</td><td>PUNCTUATION</td><td>⑨
What did he say.
What did he say?</td></tr>
<tr><td>⑩</td><td>CAPITALIZATION</td><td>⑩
I am studying english.
I am studying English.</td></tr>
<tr><td>⑪</td><td>ARTICLE</td><td>⑪
I had a accident.
I had an accident.</td></tr>
<tr><td>⑫?</td><td>MEANING NOT CLEAR</td><td>⑫?
He borrowed some smoke.
(? ? ?)</td></tr>
<tr><td>⑬</td><td>RUN-ON SENTENCE*</td><td>⑬
My roommate was sleeping, we didn't want to wake her up.
My roommate was sleeping. We didn't want to wake her up.</td></tr>
</table>

---

*A run-on sentence occurs when two sentences are incorrectly connected: the end of one sentence and the beginning of the next sentence are not properly marked by a period and a capital letter. (See Chart 9-1.)

APPENDIX 4
Basic Vocabulary List

The following list contains approximately 750 of the most commonly used words in English. *Fundamentals of English Grammar* assumes that students using this book are familiar with most of the words on the list.

The text uses many other words that are not on the list. Students may wish to add new vocabulary to this list.

The list is divided into two groups. Group One contains the most frequently used words. Group Two has other common words that the students will encounter in the text.

The words are listed according to their usual usage: NOUN, VERB, ADJECTIVE, or ADVERB.

BASIC VOCABULARY LIST: GROUP ONE

NOUNS (Group One)

accident	body	country
address	book	cup
afternoon	box	date
age	boy	daughter
air	bread	day
airplane	breakfast	desk
animal	brother	dictionary
apartment	building	dinner
arm	bus	direction
aunt	car	doctor
baby	chair	door
back	child	ear
bank	circle	earth
bed	city	end
beginning	class	evening
bicycle	clothes	eye
bird	coat	face
birthday	color*	family
boat	corner	father

---

*British English = colour

finger	movie	trouble
fire	music	uncle
fish	name	university
floor	night	vacation
food	noon	vegetable
foot	nose	vocabulary
friend	notebook	voice
front	number	wall
fruit	office	water
future	page	way
garden	parents	weather
glass	park	week
girl	part	wife
hair	party	window
half	past	woman
hand	pen	word
hat	pencil	work
head	people	world
holiday	pepper	year
home	person	zoo
homework	picture	
hospital	place	VERBS (Group One)
hotel	plant	
hour	present	answer
house	price	arrive
human being	problem	ask
husband	question	be
idea	reason	become
information	restaurant	begin
insect	rice	believe
job	river	break
juice	room	bring
land	roommate	build
language	school	buy
leg	shoe	call
letter	side	carry
library	sister	catch
life	sky	change
light	smile	close
line	son	come
lunch	sound	continue
man	street	cost
meat	student	cry
mile	sun	cut
minute	table	die
mistake	teacher	do
money	test	drink
month	thing	eat
moon	time	end
morning	town	enter
mother	tree	explain

fall
feel
fight
find
finish
fix
get
give
go
grow
happen
have
hear
help
hold
hope
hurt
interest
keep
know
laugh
learn
leave
let
like
listen
live
look
lose
love
make
mean
meet
move
need
open
pay
plan
put
rain
read
ride
run
say
see
sell
send
sit
sleep
speak
stand

start
stay
stop
study
take
talk
teach
tell
think
touch
try
turn
use
wait
walk
want
wash
watch
work
write
understand
visit

ADJECTIVES (Group One): Opposites

bad	good
beautiful	ugly
big	little
big	small
cheap	expensive
clean	dirty
cold	hot
cool	warm
dangerous	safe
dark	light
deep	shallow
different	same
difficult	simple
dry	wet
early	late
east	west
empty	full
fast	slow
fat	thin
first	last
happy	sad
hard	easy
hard	soft
healthy	ill
healthy	sick
heavy	light
high	low
intelligent	stupid
large	little
large	small
long	short
messy	neat
modern	old-fashioned
narrow	wide
noisy	quiet
north	south
old	new
old	young
poor	rich
private	public
right	left
right	wrong
rough	smooth
short	tall
sour	sweet
strong	weak

ADVERBS (Group One)

again
ago
also
always
early
ever
fast
finally
generally
hard
here
immediately
late
maybe
never
now
occasionally
often
once

BASIC VOCABULARY LIST: GROUP TWO

NOUNS (Group Two)

amount
army
art
bag
ball
beach
bill
blood
bottom
bridge
business
cat
ceiling
center*
century
chance
clock
cloud
coffee
college
computer
concert
condition
conversation
course
crowd
definition
difference
distance
dog
dress
earthquake
egg
enemy
example
experience
fact
fall/autumn
fear
field
flower
forest
form
furniture

game
gas(oline)**
gold
government
grass
group
hall
health
heart
heat
hill
history
hole
horse
hundred
ice
individual
industry
island
key
kitchen
knife
lake
law
list
luck
magazine
mail
market
math(ematics)
meaning
member
middle
midnight
milk
million
mind
mountain
mouth
nation
nature
neck
neighbor
newspaper

---

*British English = centre
**British English = petrol

noise
object
ocean
office
opinion
pain
paint
pair
pants
peace
period
picnic
pleasure
pocket
position
power
pronunciation
purpose
radio
result
ring
rule
salt
sandwich
science
sea
season
seat
shape
shirt
shoulder
situation
size
skin
snow
song
space
spelling
spring
stamp
star
store
subject
success
sugar
storm
suit
summer

tape recorder
tea
telephone
television
theater*
thousand
top
toy
train
trip
trouble
umbrella
universe
valley
value
war
wind
wing
winter
wood

VERBS (Group Two)

accept
act
add
agree
allow
appear
attempt
attend
beat
blow
borrow
burn
cause
choose
collect
complete
consider
contain
control
cook
cross
count
cover
dance
decide

disappear
discover
divide
doubt
draw
dream
dress
drive
drop
enjoy
exist
expect
fail
fill
fit
flow
fly
forget
guess
hang
hate
hit
hurry
improve
include
introduce
invite
join
kill
kiss
lead
lend
lift
marry
notice
obtain
offer
order
own
pass
permit
pick
point
pour
practice
prepare
promise
prove

---

*British English = theatre (This spelling is also frequently used in American English.)

provide
pull
push
reach
realize
receive
recognize
refuse
remember
repeat
reply
report
require
return
rise
save
search
seem
separate
serve
share
shout
show
sign
sing
smell
spell
spend
spread
succeed
suggest
supply
surprise
surround
taste
tear
thank
tie
travel
wave
wear
win
wish
wonder
worry

ADJECTIVES (Group Two)

absent
angry
bald
bright
busy
calm
dead
delicious
delightful
dizzy
essential
famous
flat
foolish
foreign
free
fresh
funny
glad
great
handsome
humid
hungry
lazy
mad
native
nervous
nice
pretty
proud
rapid
ripe
round
serious
sharp
sorry
special
strange
terrific
tough
unique
various
whole
wild
wise
wonderful

ADJECTIVE OPPOSITES

accurate	inaccurate
certain	uncertain
clear	unclear
comfortable	uncomfortable
common	uncommon
complete	incomplete
convenient	inconvenient
dependent	independent
direct	indirect
fair	unfair
familiar	unfamiliar
happy	unhappy
healthy	unhealthy
important	unimportant
interesting	uninteresting
kind	unkind
lawful	unlawful
legal	illegal
logical	illogical
necessary	unnecessary
normal	abnormal
pleasant	unpleasant
polite	impolite
possible	impossible
proper	improper
rational	irrational
real	unreal
regular	irregular
responsible	irresponsible
sure	unsure
true	untrue
usual	unusual
visible	invisible

ADVERBS (Group Two)

actually
afterward(s)
almost
already
anymore
anywhere
apparently
carefully
certainly
completely
constantly
downtown
easily
enough
entirely
especially
everywhere
extremely
fortunately
just
later
next
obviously
perhaps
quietly
rarely
regularly
seldom
seriously
somewhere
still
surely
together
too
well
yet

APPENDIX 5

Differences between American English and British English

DIFFERENCES IN VOCABULARY

Speakers of American English and speakers of British English have no trouble understanding each other. The differences are small and do not interfere with communication. Some differences in the usage of common vocabulary are listed below.

American English	British English
attorney, lawyer	barrister, solicitor
bathrobe	dressing gown
can (of beans)	tin (of beans)
cookie	biscuit
corn	maize
diaper	nappy
driver's license	driving license
drug store	chemist's
elevator	lift
eraser	rubber
flashlight	torch
gas, gasoline	petrol
hood of a car	bonnet of a car
living room	sitting room, drawing room
raise in salary	rise in salary
rest room	public toilet, WC (water closet)
schedule	timetable
sidewalk	pavement, footpath
sink	basin
soccer	football
stove	cooker
truck	lorry, van
trunk of a car	boot of a car
be on vacation	be on holiday

DIFFERENCES IN SPELLING

American English and British English have a few differences in spelling. The list below shows the spelling differences in some common words.

American English spelling	British English spelling
theater, center, liter	theatre, centre, litre
color, honor, labor, odor	colour, honour, labour, odour
jewelry, traveler, woolen	jewellry, traveller, woollen
skillful, fulfill	skilful, fulfil
check	cheque (bank note)
curb	kerb
forever	for ever/forever
jail	gaol
program	programme
specialty	speciality
story	storey (of a building)
tire	tyre (of a car)
realize, analyze, apologize	realise, analyse, apologise
defense, offense, license	defence, offence, licence (n.)
burned	burnt (*or* burned)
dreamed	dreamt (*or* dreamed)
smelled	smelt (*or* smelled)
spelled	spelt (*or* spelled)
spoiled	spoilt (*or* spoiled)

Index